Fortress • 51

Indian Castles 1206–1526

The Rise and Fall of the Delhi Sultanate

Konstantin S Nossov • Illustrated by Brian Delf

Series editors Marcus Cowper and Nikolai Bogdanovic

First published in Great Britain in 2006 by Osprey Publishing,
Midland House, West Way, Botley, Oxford OX2 0PH, UK
443 Park Avenue South, New York, NY 10016, USA
E-mail: info@ospreypublishing.com

A CIP catalogue record for this book is available from the British Library

ISBN 10: 1 84176 065 X
ISBN 13: 978 1 84176 065 9

Page layout by Ken Vail Graphic Design, Cambridge, UK
Typeset in Monotype Gill Sans and ITC Stone Serif
Maps by the Map Studio Ltd
Index by Glyn Sutcliffe
Originated by United Graphics, Singapore
Printed in China through Bookbuilders

06 07 08 09 10   10 9 8 7 6 5 4 3 2 1

For a catalogue of all books published by Osprey Military and Aviation please contact:

NORTH AMERICA
Osprey Direct, c/o Random House Distribution Center, 400 Hahn Road,
Westminster, MD 21157
E-mail: info@ospreydirect.com

ALL OTHER REGIONS
Osprey Direct UK, P.O. Box 140 Wellingborough, Northants, NN8 2FA, UK
E-mail: info@ospreydirect.co.uk

www.ospreypublishing.com

Artist's note

Readers may care to note that the original paintings from which
the colour plates in this book were prepared are available for
private sale. All reproduction copyright whatsoever is retained by
the Publishers. All enquiries should be addressed to:

Mr Brian Delf
7 Burcot Park
Burcot
Abingdon,
OX14 3DH
UK.

The Publishers regret that they can enter into no correspondence
upon this matter.

Acknowledgements

The author wishes to express sincere thanks to Vladimir V.
Golubev who supplied all the black and white pictures for
this book.

Author's note

For the sake of convenience in reading, the author uses a
simplified version of spelling for Sanskrit words in the main text.
In the glossary, however, a more precise spelling is given in
parentheses.
There are two ways of referring to the ancient Indian text
The Arthashastra: the first indicating the book and the chapter; the
second, the section and the chapter. For the sake of convenience a
combination of the two is used in this book: first comes the book,
then the chapter and finally the section in parentheses.
All the photographs in this book are from the author's collection.
All requests should be addressed to: konst-nosov@mtu-net.ru.

Sanskrit linear measurements

1 angula – 1.9cm
1 aratni – 0.45m
1 danda – 1.8m
1 yojana – 14.63km
1 krosha – 3.66km
1 hasta – 0.45m

The Fortress Study Group (FSG)

The object of the FSG is to advance the education of the public
in the study of all aspects of fortifications and their armaments,
especially works constructed to mount or resist artillery. The FSG
holds an annual conference in September over a long weekend
with visits and evening lectures, an annual tour abroad lasting
about eight days, and an annual Members' Day.
The FSG journal *FORT* is published annually, and its newsletter
Casemate is published three times a year. Membership is
international. For further details, please contact:
The Secretary, c/o 6 Lanark Place, London W9 1BS, UK

Contents

Introduction

By the end of the 1st millennium AD constant wars between the different kingdoms of Hindustan made the country vulnerable to outside attack. Early in the 11th century northern India found itself the object of ruinous raids by several Muslim-Turkic rulers. The first of them worth mentioning is Mahmud of Ghazni, who made 17 raids on India during his rule (998–1030). The next significant figure was Muhammad of Ghur (r.1173–1206), who conquered northern India and established control over areas earlier dominated by the Rajputs. Muhammad of Ghur was succeeded by his slave, Qutb-ud-din Aibak (r.1206–10), who founded the first of the five Muslim dynasties, collectively known as the Delhi Sultanate. He made Delhi (then known as Dhillika or Dhilli) his capital and laid the foundations of the famous Qutb Minar complex. Throughout the 13th century the Mongols made frequent raids on northern India and the Delhi sultans were so involved in opposing them that expanding the borders of the sultanate was almost impossible.

Between 1290 and 1320 the sultanate was ruled by the Khalji dynasty. Ala-ud-din (r.1296–1316) substantially expanded the territory of the Delhi Sultanate; his power extended westward as far as the Indus River and eastward as far as Varanasi. The Deccan and southern Indian states had to acknowledge the Khalji overlords and pay tribute to the sultanate. Only Bengal in the east was governed by independent rulers. The Khaljis were succeeded by the Tughluq dynasty that was in power from 1320 to 1414. The second ruler from this dynasty, Muhammad bin Tughluq, completed the conquest of the Deccan and southern India, and annexed them to the Delhi Sultanate. However, many provinces rose in revolt, partly in response to the lax control of the sultans. As early as 1336 the Hindu Vijayanagar Empire proclaimed independence in south India, and the Muslim Bahmani kingdom was formed in the Deccan in 1347. The Mongol conqueror Timur inflicted a severe blow on the Tughluq dynasty when he invaded India and completely destroyed Delhi in 1398. A number of independent kingdoms emerged early in the 15th century: Mandu in 1401, Gujarat in 1407 and Jaunpur in 1408. Several independent Rajput kingdoms appeared in Rajasthan, the most important being Mewar and Marwar.

Fortifications of the Urwahi Gate of Gwalior Castle. The gate itself is screened by the barbican and cannot be seen from this distance. Beyond it the road climbs up the gorge and an unwanted visitor would find himself under flanking fire from the walls on both sides of the gorge.

Many Muslim invaders came to India with fixed ideas about military architecture and they employed perfect siege weapons. In carrying out their policy of aggression, the Delhi sultans sought to subjugate rather than devastate newly conquered territories. They could not afford to leave castles in the hands of rebellious subjects, however, and had to lay sieges in order to capture the castles and complete their control over a region. On overcoming Hindu castles, they would destroy the temples and erect mosques. The invaders were more tolerant with regard to fortifications, whether for reasons of economy or because they recognized the effectiveness of Hindu military architecture. As a rule, they were content to restore those parts of a castle that had been destroyed during a siege, and it is still possible to see the occasional gate that was rebuilt in the Muslim style among the traditional gates of a Hindu castle.

Badalgarh or the Hindola Gate, the second gate from the bottom of the north-east gate complex of Gwalior Castle. Built in the late-15th century, the gate is an excellent example of Hindu architecture.

The Delhi sultans of the 13th and 14th centuries were military leaders who spent most of their lives on the march. Being extremely ambitious and vainglorious, they wished to be remembered by generations to come. Not only did they win one victory after another, but they also built sumptuous tombs for themselves as permanent memorials. Their capitals were built on the territory of the modern city of Delhi, with every new fortified town erected on a bare plot of land and inhabited by citizens moved from the older city that was only a few kilometres away. These cities sometimes existed for no more than a few years before they were abandoned. Muhammad bin Tughluq excelled all the others in this respect. He added the Adilabad Fortress to the newly built Tughluqabad in 1325, only to move all the inhabitants into a new city, Jahanpanah, a few years later. In 1328 he transferred his capital to Daulatabad, forcing the residents to cover a distance of 1,127km. Nine years later he returned his capital to Dhillika (Delhi), but thousands of those who accompanied him did not survive the journey.

Muslim military architecture differed considerably from the Hindu style, both in design (the shape of arches and vaults, for example) and elements of decor. Sometimes extremely utilitarian, even severe as in Tughluqabad, Muslim fortification merged over time with Hindu influences, giving rise to a new, Hindu–Muslim style. As the dominance of the Delhi sultans expanded further south, so too, did the impact of Muslim architecture. While Muslim architecture gained a firm hold in the Deccan, it did not win recognition in the extreme south of Hindustan where, as in Rajasthan in western India, fortifications were still built in the Hindu style.

The last two dynasties of the Delhi Sultanate, the Sayyids (1414–51) and the Lodis (1451–1526), were involved in incessant civil disorder. By the 15th–early 16th centuries the borders of the Delhi Sultanate were dramatically reduced: it now covered the Punjab, the province of Delhi and the valley of the Ganges and Yamuna. The situation attracted the attention of Babur, ruler of Fergana. Between 1518 and 1526 Babur invaded India five times. Finally, on 21 April 1526 he routed the army of the Delhi Sultan Ibrahim Lodi at the battle of Panipat. A few days later Babur took Agra (the capital of the Lodi dynasty since 1502) and Delhi without a single shot. Babur was a Mongul, or *Mughul* in Persian, and his victory marked the end of the Delhi Sultanate and the beginning of the Mughal Empire.

The decline of the Delhi Sultanate in the 15th century led to a sudden growth in the number of castles. Feudal divisions led to a situation where each lord needed to fortify his province with numerous castles. It was a period when Indian castles obtained their characteristic outline that would later be only modified to meet new requirements of siege warfare.

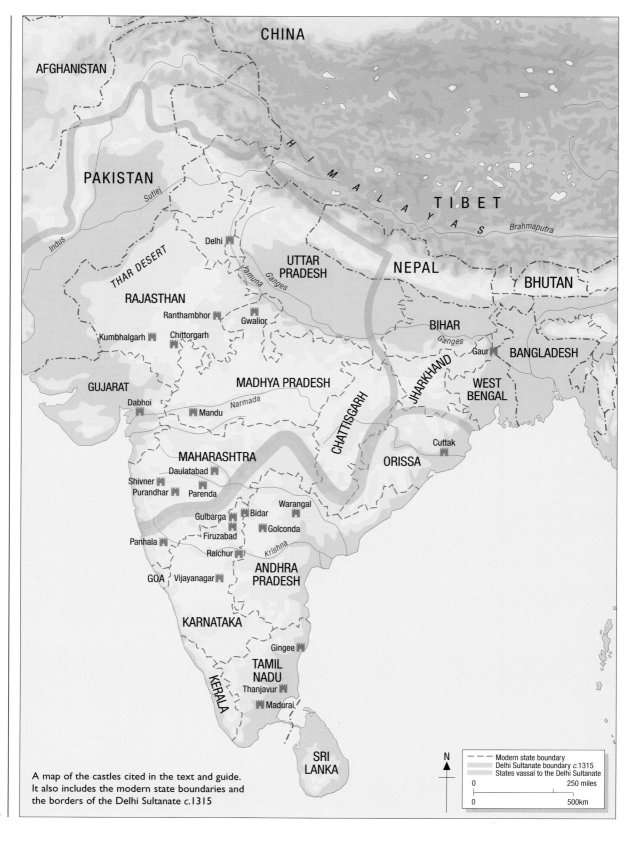

CHINA

AFGHANISTAN

PAKISTAN

Sutlej

Indus

THAR DESERT

RAJASTHAN

Delhi

UTTAR
PRADESH

Yamuna

Ganges

HIMALAYAS

TIBET

Brahmaputra

NEPAL

BHUTAN

Ranthambhor

Gwalior

Kumbhalgarh

Chittorgarh

GUJARAT

MADHYA PRADESH

Dabhoi

Narmada

Mandu

BIHAR

Ganges

JHARKHAND

Gaur

BANGLADESH

WEST
BENGAL

CHATTISGARH

ORISSA

Cuttak

MAHARASHTRA

Daulatabad

Shivner

Purandhar

Parenda

Gulbarga

Bidar

Warangal

Firuzabad

Golconda

Panhala

Raichur

Krishna

GOA

Vijayanagar

ANDHRA
PRADESH

KARNATAKA

Gingee

TAMIL
NADU

KERALA

Thanjavur

Madurai

SRI
LANKA

N

Modern state boundary
Delhi Sultanate boundary *c.*1315
States vassal to the Delhi Sultanate

0   250 miles

0   500km

A map of the castles cited in the text and guide.
It also includes the modern state boundaries and
the borders of the Delhi Sultanate *c.*1315

Chronology

1206	Assassination of Muhammad of Ghur, Afghan ruler who had conquered northern India. His vicegerent in India, Ghulam (Arabic for 'slave') Qutb-ud-din Aibak, declared his independence and founded the first Muslim dynasty of the Delhi Sultanate, the so-called Slave dynasty
1206–10	Rule of Qutb-ud-din Aibak
1206–90	Rule of the Slave dynasty
1210–36	Rule of Iltutmish, who managed to unite the whole of northern India, from the Indus valley in the west to the lower reaches of the Ganges in the east, under the control of the Delhi Sultanate
1221	The first appearance of the Mongols in India when they sacked western Punjab, Sind and northern Gujarat
1241	Mongol invaders captured Lahore, killing nearly all its inhabitants and levelling the town walls to the ground
1246	The Mongols took Uch and Multan
1266–87	Rule of Balban who consolidated central power, put down armed uprisings and repelled several Mongol invasions
1290–96	Rule of Jalal-ud-din Firuz Shah who founded the Khalji dynasty
1290–1301	Several campaigns to seize Ranthambhor Castle, which was finally captured by Ala-ud-din Khalji in 1301
1290–1320	Rule of the Khalji dynasty
1292	Another Mongol invasion
1294	Ala-ud-din Khalji, the nephew of Firuz Shah, marched to the Deccan and returned with huge booty
1296–1316	Rule of Ala-ud-din Khalji who managed to subjugate all Hindustan with the exception of Bengal
1297–1307	The Mongols invaded several times and threatened Delhi, but Ala-ud-din Khalji repeatedly beat them back. 1308 marks the end of Mongol incursions into the territory of the Sultanate territory
1300–01	Siege of Ranthambhor Castle by the army of Ala-ud-din Khalji.
1303	Ala-ud-din Khalji builds Siri, a new, so-called second city of Delhi. Chittorgarh besieged by Ala-ud-din Khalji
1305	Ala-ud-din Khalji conquered Malwa
1307–11	Malik Kafur, a general and slave of Ala-ud-din Khalji, led a campaign in the Deccan and southern India
1320	Ghiyath-ud-din Tughluq, a commander in Ala-ud-din Khalji's army, seized the throne of the Delhi Sultanate
1320–1414	Rule of the Tughluq dynasty
1320–25	Rule of Ghiyath-ud-din Tughluq, who built Tughluqabad, the third city of Delhi, as well as a splendid tomb for himself near the fortress
1325–51	Rule of Muhammad bin Tughluq, the builder of Delhi's fourth city, Jahanpanah, and erector of a new fortress, Adilabad, near the town-fortress of Tughluqabad
1328	Muhammad bin Tughluq transferred the capital from Delhi to Daulatabad
1334–78	Muslim kingdom of Madurai founded in the extreme south of Hindustan
1336	Vijayanagar Empire founded in the south of Hindustan
1337	Delhi became the capital of the Delhi sultans again
1347	Bahmani kingdom founded in the west of the central Deccan.
1351–88	Rule of Firuz Shah Tughluq, who built Delhi's fifth city (Firuzabad)
1388–1414	Decay of the Delhi Sultanate. Many provinces declared their independence.
1398–99	Timur invaded India. A terrible carnage in Delhi and many other towns of north-western India
1414–51	Rule of the Sayyid dynasty, whose power remained weak
1451–1526	Rule of the Lodi dynasty
1482–1512	Bahmani kingdom disintegrated into separate Muslim kingdoms of Ahmadnagar, Golconda, Berar and Bidar
1498	Arrival of the Portuguese squadron led by Vasco da Gama
1526	Babur defeated the last Delhi sultan, Ibrahim Lodi, in the battle of Panipat; end of the Delhi Sultanate and the foundation of the Mughal Empire

The principles of defence

Fort, castle or fortress?

In India the words 'castle' and 'fortress' are not commonly used. All old fortifications are referred to as forts: they include the Red Fort at Delhi, the Red Fort at Agra, Ranthambhor Fort and Gwalior Fort. The exceptional usage of the term 'fort' dates back to the era of British rule. In the 17th–19th centuries castles became a thing of the past in Britain and Europe, leaving the word 'fort' as the main and indeed the only name for closed fortification structures. The British therefore called any fortification 'fort' whether Europeans or Indians had built it.

Today, however, historians draw a clear distinction between 'forts', 'castles' and 'fortresses'. A fort is a comparatively small military structure closed on each side and housing a limited number of inhabitants, usually a military garrison. A castle, however, is a fortified residence of a feudal lord and his subjects. The fairly widespread term 'fortress' most often implies a strong permanent closed fortification occupying a large area, which may include a town. Sometimes the word 'fortress' is used for any formidable fortification, but a fortress considerably surpasses a fort in size. Most surviving fortification structures of medieval India come closest to the notion of 'castle'. As in Europe, castles in India served as dwellings for feudal lords and combined both beauty and practicality in their construction; many functioned as palaces and remain much admired by tourists. However, most Indian castles occupy a substantial territory and therefore can be classified as fortresses. In this book, departing from Indian tradition, the term 'castle' will be used in the first place; 'fortress' will be used to refer to especially large castles and to deal with the general theories of construction and defence.

The Sanskrit words for castles or fortresses are *durga* or *durg*. *Durga* also means 'a place of difficult access', which suggests that a wide range of natural obstacles, such as mountains, rivers, etc., were taken into consideration when erecting a fortress. The Sanskrit term *pura* is less frequently used for fortresses. The Hindi word for fortress or castle is *qila*; in Rajasthan, Assam and some other districts they are called *garh*.

Types of castle

Ancient and medieval Indian treatises (*shastras*) abound with descriptions of various types of fortresses. The most famous of these treatises is *The Arthashastra*, probably written by the statesman Kautilya somewhere between the end of the 4th century BC and the 1st–2nd centuries AD. Most *shastras* were written in the 1st millennium AD, although there are exceptions from earlier or later periods. The *shastras* discuss many aspects of statesmanship and give advice to rulers; they also describe six principal types of Indian fortress.

Jala-durga is a fortress surrounded by water, also known as *audaka-durga* and *ab-durga*. There are two subtypes – the island fortress, or *antardvipa-durga*, and the plain fortress or *sthala-durga*. The sea or the waters of a river wash the first, while the latter is encircled with artificial moats filled with water or irrigated by a river. Plain fortresses are naturally much more common.

Giri-durga, or *parvata-durga*, is a hill or mountain fortress. There are three varieties: *prantara-durga*, *giri-parshva-durga* and *guha-durga*. *Prantara-durga* is a fortress built on the summit (usually flat) of a hill or a mountain. This was the most common type in the Middle Ages, and the best examples are the castles of Gwalior, Chittor and Ranthambhor. In *giri-parshva-durga* both major civilian structures and fortifications extend down the slope of a hill or mountain,

though the summit is certainly included into the defence system, too. The living quarters of a *guha-durga* fortress are situated in a valley surrounded by high, impassable hills. The hills house a chain of outposts and signal towers connected by extensive defensive walls.

Dhanvana, dhanva, dhanu-durga or *maru-durga* are desert fortresses, usually to be found in an arid area bare of trees, grass or sources of water over a distance of no less than 5 yojanas (73km), hence its other name, *nirudaka-durga*, or waterless fortress. An *airina-durga* is built on saline soil of barren tract or on fens impregnated with saline water and protected by the thorny bushes that grow there.

A *vana-durga* or *vrikshya-durga*, or arboreal fortress, would be surrounded on all sides with a dense, impassable forest over a distance of at least 4 kroshas (14.6km). Variations were the *khanjana-durga*, built on fens and encircled with thorny woods, and the *sthambha-durga*, erected in the jungles among high trees but lacking sufficient sources of water.

There are three types of *mahi-durga* or earth fortress: *mrid-durga, panka-durga* and *parigha-durga*. *Mrid-durga* are encircled with earthen walls; the approaches to *panka-durga* are protected by fens or quicksand; and *parigha-durga* are surrounded by walls made of earth and stone or brick, their height exceeding 12 cubits (5.4m) and their width constituting half of the height.

Nri-durga, or 'fortress with men', was defended by a large and loyal army of proven warriors, and was well supplied with arms. It was usually a city fortress, well populated with a substantial garrison. It was also called *nara-durga* and *bala-durga*.

One fortress could combine the defensive features of two or even three types of castle. Ranthambhor Castle, for example, stands on a hill (*giri-durga*) and used to be surrounded by dense forests (*vana-durga*). When a considerable garrison of soldiers was billeted in it, the castle could also be classified as *nri-durga*.

Each type of fortress had different advantages. According to Manu, a mountain fortress (*giri-durga*) was the best defensive structure, and some Sanskrit texts state that the gods chose to make their abode in these places. It is interesting that nearly all castles with the names ending in *garh* are mountain or hill castles. Mountains formed of horizontal bedding rock were seismically safe and served as an excellent foundation for heavy stone structures. Manu also considers the disadvantages of other fortresses. A fortress surrounded by water often sheltered reptiles and snakes, which made for a rapid spread of disease; on the other hand, reptiles and snakes could deter an assault on a fortress, and disease could force the enemy to lift a siege. Earth fortresses often swarmed with rats and rodents, which might in the long run eat away their foundations. Monkeys plagued the inhabitants of arboreal fortresses, while a fortress that housed a lot of people had to be kept well supplied with food and water to feed all those mouths. Other sources, however, such as the *Mahabharata* epic, believe that *nri-durga*, or garrisoned forts, were the most effective.

A north-west view of Ranthambhor Castle. The castle sits on the flat summit of a hill, towering 213m above the surrounding valley. The castle walls, reinforced with semicircular towers, edge the hill, following its outline. The castle may be described as a hill fortress (*giri-durga* type), but it was once enclosed by dense forests, and could have been referred to as an arboreal fortress (*vana-durga* type).

Gwalior Castle, the 10th–17th centuries

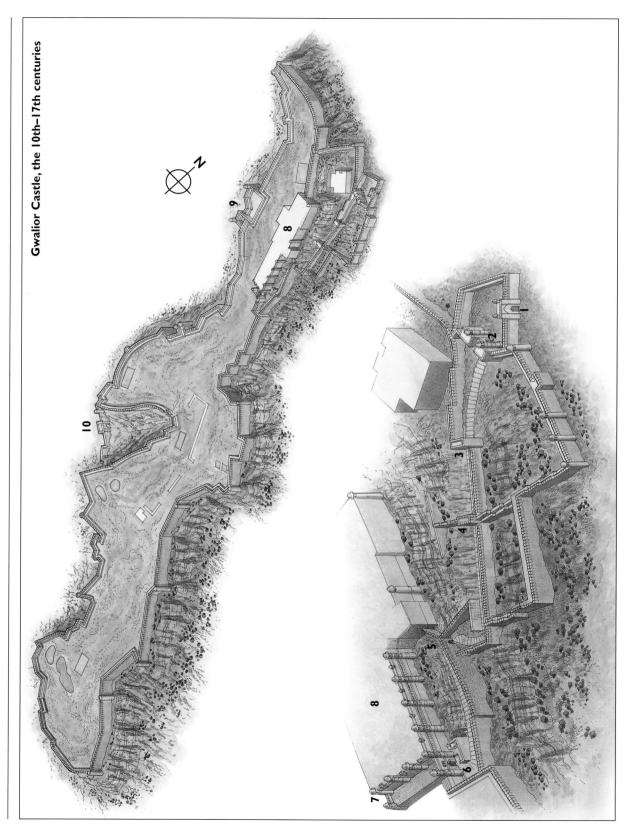

LEFT **Gwalior Castle, the 10th–17th centuries**

Exactly when Gwalior Castle was constructed is unknown; it undoubtedly existed in the 10th century but it might have been built as early as the beginning of the 6th century AD. It changed hands more than once and saw many sieges. Its fortifications were rebuilt several times and one can now see fortifications dating from the 10th to the 17th centuries. The castle has three main entrances. The north-east gate complex, shown in the inset, is the most interesting one. A winding road leads up here, which used to be barred with seven gates, of which only five survive. The first from the bottom, Alamgiri Gate (**1**), was built in 1660 and named after the Mughal emperor Aurangzeb. The second up the road, Badalgarh or Hindola Gate (**2**), was constructed in the late-15th century and is an excellent example of Hindu architecture; it has something in common with the sixth, Hathi Gate (**6**), and Man Mandir Palace. The third, Bhairon or Bansor Gate (**3**), erected by Bhairon Pal of the Kachhwaha dynasty, does not survive. The fourth from the bottom, Ganesh Gate (**4**), was built in mid-15th century in a simple, unsophisticated Hindu style. Of even simpler appearance is the fifth, Lakshman Gate (**5**), built in AD 970 but undoubtedly repaired later, when some of the stones were reset upside-down, with the sculptured faces upon them inverted. The sixth and most beautiful gate is called Hathi, or Elephant Gate (**6**), because a statue of an elephant with a drover on it used to stand here. Behind the gate there was a long passage leading to the last, seventh gate now destroyed. It owed its name, Hawa, or Wind Gate (**7**), to the draught of cool air that wafted into the passage and refreshed everyone who had come a long and difficult way up the serpentine road. Next to the Elephant Gate stands Man Mandir (**8**), the finest of the six palaces of Gwalior Castle. The north-west entrance (**9**) has three gates, which are collectively called the Dhonda Gates as they were built at the time of Dhonda Deva, an early Kachhwaha ruler. The south-west entrance (**10**) is situated in a gorge and called the Urwahi Gate.

The six types of fortress described above were considered fundamental, although other systems of classification have noted different types. One occasionally comes across very exotic names whose meaning can only be guessed at. For example, in the treatise of *Manasara Shilpashastra*, which is thought to date back to the 10th–11th centuries, eight types of fortresses are mentioned: *sibira* or *shivira*, *vahinimukha*, *sthaniya*, *dronaka* or *dronamukha*, *samviddha* or *vardhaka*, *kolaka* or *kolumkolaka*, *nigama* and *skandhavara*. They were subdivided according to their location into several subtypes: *giri-durga* (hill or mountain fortress), *ratha-durga* (chariot fortress), *deva-durga* (gods' fortress), *panka-durga* (marsh fortress) and *mishra-durga* (mixed fortress). A large body of chariots probably protected the chariot fortress, although chariots had long since disappeared from Indian armies. The name 'gods' fortress' is difficult to interpret. Mountain fortresses were believed to be the home of the gods, but here mountain fortresses and gods' fortresses are differentiated. The same treatise names three types of fortified towns: *padmaka* – a round or square town surrounded by a ditch and a solid wall containing 8, 12 or 16 gates, provided with various war engines and troops and having an inexhaustible source of water; *svastika* – a rectangular town; *karmuka* – a semicircular town.

A wall of Qila Rai Pithora or the first city of Delhi, built c.1180. Laid entirely of rubble, the walls are 5–6m thick in places.

The ancient text *Vishvakarma Vastu Shastra* offers another approach. Out of the 12 types of fortress, the first four are the already familiar hill or mountain, arboreal, water and desert fortresses. The fifth to eighth types include fortresses on the bank of a river or a sea shore, which are named according to the number of gates, the fifth type being a one-gate fortress (*ekamukha-durga*), the sixth a two-gate fortress (*dwimukha-durga*) and so on. The ninth type, the tortoise fortress (*kurma-durga*) was built in the forest or at the foot of a hill and was probably used to launch ambushes. The tenth type is another *parvata-durga*, though not the same as a hill fortress as it is placed separately for a reason, its exact purpose is unknown. The eleventh type, *prabha-durga*, is a formidable fortress protected by several rings of walls and watchtowers. The twelfth type, *ayudha-durga*, is a fortress well equipped for both defence and offence with all the necessary structures and weapons.

Methods of construction

Stone was the main material for building fortifications in medieval India. Walls were erected by one of the following three construction methods. A wall could be an earthen rampart faced with stone on both sides. The rampart was built using the earth excavated while digging the ditch, with three-quarters of it used for building a rampart and one-quarter for levelling out the surface inside the fortress and in front of the ditch. Facing the rampart with stone allowed for the erection of higher and steeper walls than those possible with a purely earthen rampart. The structure had a substantial shortcoming, however: an earthen core accumulated water, which could destroy the stone shell. Drainage channels were therefore installed along the length of the wall from top to bottom.

The second method consisted of filling the space between the outer layers with earth mixed with rubble. This core was considerably harder than simply using rammed earth. The third and most advanced method involved the use of mortar. A rubble-built wall fastened with mortar was strong and long lasting. Construction methods depended, however, on the materials available.

As a rule, walls were faced with ashlar (stones or bricks) free of mortar, as in the citadel of Golconda. Sometimes the whole wall, together with the outer layers, was laid with arbitrary-shaped rubble fastened with mortar. This type of structure may be seen in the fortifications of Qila Rai Pithora, the so-called first city of Delhi.

The fifth gate (Jorla Pol) of the western gate complex in Chittorgarh. It is the only gate of the complex obviously rebuilt by Muslims. Muslim influence is particularly evident in the pointed arch. In all the other gates the heads of the passages are constructed with flat lintels and corbels, which is characteristic of Hindu architecture.

The re-use of existing materials from destroyed buildings is characteristic of fortifications built in a hurry. In erecting the walls of Banbeer in Chittorgarh during the siege of 1534–35 extensive use was made of columns, stones of different size and colour, and decorative slabs. In this case columns were used as an important form of horizontal bonding.

While it was characteristic of Hindu architecture to overlap the heads of passages with flat lintels on corbels, Muslim influence is clear in the appearance of regular and often pointed arches. The construction of such arches became possible when they learnt to lay bricks and stones in a fan shape, which secured an arch. Regular arches did not oust traditional Hindu lintels and corbels except in areas where Muslim influence was especially strong. Many castles that were only temporarily occupied by Muslim conquerors display a combination of Hindu and Muslim architectural styles. All the gates of the western entrance to Chittorgarh are constructed with flat lintels and corbels, except for the fifth, Jorla Pol, which has a pointed arch and has undoubtedly been rebuilt by Muslims. The spread of Muslim rule added another characteristic feature to military architecture – vast domes over square structures. The third gate (Gumbad Gate) of the Triple Gate in Bidar is a fine example.

Great importance was attached to the appearance of fortifications. Not only were they intended to overwhelm a visitor with the power and wealth of the ruler, but they were also intended to impress him with their beauty and grace. Much attention was paid to the decor of the fortifications, especially the gate, which was the first point of entrance. *Vishvakarma* says that both the walls and gates should be embossed with the emblem of the capital: a flag, sword, warrior, lion, elephant or horse. Sculptures or reliefs of lions, tigers, elephants or mystic animals were frequently placed on either side of a gateway, such as those at the western gate to the citadel of Warangal, as well as on the Sharza Gate in Bidar. The life-sized sculpture of an elephant ridden by a drover used to stand in front of the sixth gate of the north-eastern entrance to Gwalior Castle, which explains why the gate was called Hathi or Elephant Gate. Gates or nearby towers were sometimes covered with relief representations of scenes of dances or battle as high as a man's height, such as the seventh (Ram Pol) gate of the western entrance to Chittorgarh. Floral ornamental design and decorative rosettes, like those on the Bala Hisar Gate in Golconda, were also common.

The upper part of the Bala Hisar Gate leading to the citadel of Golconda. Its decor includes reliefs of lions and peacocks, round rosettes and floral ornaments.

Castle design and development

Walls, towers and gates are an integral part of nearly every medieval castle. Only the simplest fortifications may lack towers, but this is not the case of medieval Indian fortifications. Most Indian castles have a ditch, dry or filled with water, in front of the walls; only mountain castles rarely have a ditch. To make up for it, the slopes of the mountains were scarped to make them steeper.

Ditches

In *The Arthashastra*, Kautilya (Art. II, 3 (21)) recommends surrounding a fortress with three ditches (*parikha*) filled with water. Their width was to be 14, 12 and 10 danda (25.2, 21.6 and 18m respectively), their depth should be one-quarter or half of the width, with width at the bottom equal to one-third of the width at the top. The ditches were to be at a distance of 1 danda (1.8m) from each other.

This was an ideal scheme but it was rarely put into practice. In some places, such as Bidar, the upper town was protected in the most vulnerable places by a triple moat. In most cases, however, there was only one ditch.

A ditch could be dry or filled with water. In early medieval castles a ditch was often left empty, although Kautilya advised facing it with stone or brick. The moat was connected to a river, a natural spring, or a deep well in order to fill it. Drainage systems were often connected to moats, which meant that sewage could be taken out of the castle, while water could also be taken from the moat. Castles were sometimes positioned next to a river so that it could be used as a moat. The triple moat on the southern part of the upper town in Bidar is partitioned with cross-walls that form dams. A system of sluices ensured control over the water level in the moat so that it could be flooded as much as necessary.

Water-filled moats were filled with plants such as lotuses, lilies and creepers. Although they softened the severe appearance of fortifications, they also served a practical purpose by making it far more difficult for attackers to cross. Animals were used in a similar way: specially bred crocodiles and poisonous snakes were a real danger to anybody who found himself in the waters of some moats. Dry ditches would be strewn with sharp objects, often bamboo shoots cut at an acute angle.

The walls of Gwalior Castle at the Urwahi Gate. The walls run along the edge of the precipice, and even project over it in places. The slopes of the hill were cut off to make them steeper. A parapet with semicircular and slightly pointed merlons, characteristic of Indian fortification, can be seen in the foreground.

The upper and lower towns of Bidar are separated by formidable fortifications and a triple moat. On both sides and in the middle, the moats are partitioned by sluices that control the water level. Shown here is the eastern end of the triple moat. The central moat closes with a squat tower, which allowed flanking fire along the moat and prevented an assault along the cross-wall.

The ground in front of the ditch was often planted with low, thorny bushes. They provided no protection to those in attack, and actually impeded their advance by turning them into a good target. Pitfalls strewn with sharp objects were sometimes hidden in the bushes.

The wall was raised either from the bottom of a ditch or a few steps away from it. In the first case, the inner side of the ditch was faced with stone, which prevented attackers digging an underground tunnel under a dry ditch. In the second case, a small horizontal strip of land, known as a berm, was left between the ditch and the wall. Berms prevented the soil from crumbling and the wall slipping into the ditch. The width of the berm depended on the soil – the harder the soil, the narrower the berm. Both variants are present in Bidar: the outer wall in the north-west section of the upper town rises straight from the bottom of the ditch, while the southern wall of the upper town is separated from the moat with a small berm 0.3 to 1m wide.

Walls

Walls (*prakara* or *shala*) of Indian castles often seem higher from the outside than from the inside. In mountain and hill castles such as Chittorgarh and Tughluqabad, this impression is created because the scarped slopes of the rock were faced with stone. The lower part of the wall is not actually a wall proper – the masonry conceals natural rock. This construction had a number of advantages

The Kalyani Gate in Bidar, on the western side of the upper town, which is particularly well fortified. The wall is fronted by a triple ditch; this photograph has been taken from its bottom. Two rocky walls partition the ditch and were deliberately left behind after excavating the ditches. It is obvious that this section of the ditch was never filled with water, as the road runs along its bottom. It then turns left at a right angle, rounds the tower, climbs up the steps and goes through the tower (on the left), and finally gives on to another, inner gate.

The walls of Chittorgarh seen from the western side. They follow the outline of the hill as if growing out of the rock. The walls are lower on the inside than on the outside because their lower part is just rock faced with stone.

over the more common style where inner and outer walls were of equal height: they are less labour intensive to build and almost invincible against siege weapons – battering rams, borers and undermining were all useless against these walls. Castles in open countryside, such as Bidar, were reinforced in a similar way by building a gently sloping earthen embankment inside the fortress, using the earth excavated from the ditch. On the whole, however, the difference in height between the internal and external sides of walls in plain fortresses was smaller than in mountain or hill fortresses.

Some castles of the period had two lines of walls running parallel to each other, although on the whole this was a later practice, when the role of plain castles had increased. The inner wall was always higher than the outer to enable the defenders to fire over the heads of their colleagues on the outer wall onto the attackers, thus doubling the available firepower. If the outer wall was breached, the defenders on the inner wall had a good chance of dislodging the attackers from the outer wall due to their height advantage. *Vishvakarma* recommends that the inner wall be made a quarter higher than the outer. In practice, however, this was rarely achieved, with only Tughluqabad possessing walls built to this ratio. The distance between the inner and outer walls varied greatly. While the gap is only 1.5–2m in Tughluqabad, it reaches about 5m on the stretch between the Delhi Gate and the citadel in Bidar. The space between the walls was often filled with soil up to the level of the parapet of the outer wall. As a rule, this was accounted for by the structure of the wall itself. With the wall-walk of the outer wall situated on a level with the top of the hill, and the lower part of the wall just a slope faced with stone, the inner wall starts on the level of the wall-walk of the outer wall.

A gallery frequently ran along the thickness of a wall. With its loopholes forming the lower tier of fire, the gallery often opened out onto the inside with numerous arches, and was sometimes divided into small compartments by cross-walls. Guards rested in them and they allowed the besieged to localize a possible breach during an attack. This structure can be seen in the walls of Tughluqabad and Adilabad. However, in the surviving section of the wall of Siri, the second city of Delhi, there are two mural galleries, but they have no arches on the inner side. The roof of the upper gallery formed a wall-walk.

Towers

Most of the towers, or *attalaka*, on Indian castles were semicircular, resembling a letter 'D' in layout. As a rule they were fairly squat, which is why they are often called bastions, but strictly speaking this term should only be applied to the later, arrow-headed projections on bastioned traced fortifications. Round,

A fragment of the wall of Siri or the second city of Delhi. There were two mural galleries matching the two rows of loopholes in the photograph. The parapet does not survive, but it probably included two more tiers of fire, one in merlons and crenels, and the other through the loopholes directed downward from the parapet.

square or polygonal (hexagonal and octagonal) towers were comparatively rare. Castle towers, particularly circular and semicircular towers, usually had a wide base that grew narrower towards the top, giving them a cone shape. Some towers barely projected beyond the line of the wall, but in other cases almost the whole tower stuck out.

In many hill and mountain castles towers were irregularly positioned along castle walls; they were placed close together in the most vulnerable places and further apart where the terrain provided natural obstacles. If a wall conformed to the outline of a mountain or a hill, and its curve or projection could provide a position for enfilade fire, then there was no need for an extra tower.

In castles situated on plains or low hills, towers were distributed more regularly along the walls. The distance between them did not exceed 100m and was usually 30–50m, which allowed double flanking fire to be brought to bear upon the space between them.

As a rule, a tower was the same height as the adjoining curtain wall or, rarely, slightly higher. The lower part, like the lower part of the wall, was often the stone-faced slope of a mountain or a hill. Even in plain country fortresses, towers were generally half filled with rubble or earth and usually had only two storeys: the lower one with loopholes and the upper one situated on a level with the battlemented parapet. There were even one-storey towers with a fighting platform on parapet level.

Some walls and towers had a solid talus, or sloping base. This was not a load-bearing part of the structure, but it greatly increased the thickness of a wall or tower at the base. Besides adding to the strength of fortifications, these structures provided substantial protection against battering rams, the destruction of a wall at its foot and even against undermining, as the enemy would have to dig down to a great depth to make any progress. A thick, high talus also hindered escalades, as scaling ladders had to be placed at a considerable distance from the wall. The greater the angle between the scaling ladder and the wall, the longer the ladder needed to be; and the longer the scaling ladder, the greater the chance of it breaking under the weight of the attackers. It was already common knowledge that scaling ladders longer than 10m were unsafe, and assaults from such ladders were often ineffective. In addition, stones thrown from the walls could ricochet off the talus, inflicting serious casualties on an enemy.

The talus probably appeared in Indian military architecture as a result of Muslim influence. One of the best is clearly visible at the base of the walls and towers of Tughluqabad, the third city of Delhi, built in 1321–25. It was probably used to deter escalade attacks and to deflect stones thrown from above. The lower part of the walls is just a rocky outcrop faced with stone, and attacks with siege

engines or sapping were unlikely. The towers have a substantial talus, while that on the walls is considerably less solid. This forced the enemy to storm the curtain wall instead of a tower, thus exposing them to flanking fire from the towers.

The talus was never widespread in India, possibly because its advantages did not justify the labour costs. Whatever the reason, other Delhi fortresses, built either before Tughluqabad (Lal Kot, Qila Rai Pithora, Siri) or immediately after (Jahanpanah, Firuz Shah Kotla), had no talus. Nor do we find one in most other Indian castles. Only the towers of Kumbhalgarh, which was built in the mid-15th century, can boast a solid and complicated talus. While the talus of Tughluqabad slants downward comparatively evenly, in Kumbhalgarh its slope is nearly vertical along the lower part of the talus, after which the angle alters abruptly. The talus was primarily intended to prevent escalade by extending the distance between the foot of a scaling ladder and the tower.

Gates

Great attention was always paid to the defence of the entrances to a castle. Gates (*gopura*, *pratoli*, *darvaza* or *pol*) were generally cut in a wall and flanked by towers. More rarely, they were incorporated in a low gate tower; often it was not even a tower proper, but a curtain wall a little higher than the rest of the wall.

To strengthen the defences of the most important sections, several gates were set one after another. Traditionally, there should be seven gates at the main entrance to a Rajput castle, although in reality there were often fewer. Mountain castles and those sitting on high hills had the greatest number of gates, often positioned along an ascending, serpentine road. There are seven gates at the main western entrance to Chittorgarh, four gates at the eastern entrance, and only one gate at the northern. In Gwalior Castle there used to be seven gates at the north-eastern entrance, three at the north-western, and two at the south-

ABOVE The walls of Kumbalgarh embrace a vast area of several square kilometres. Semicircular D-shaped towers are as high as the walls and have only one storey – a fighting platform on a level with battlemented parapet. The wall-walk is so wide that six horsemen are said to have been able to ride abreast along it.

RIGHT The walls of the citadel of Tughluqabad. The walls and towers are reinforced with a solid talus. Two rows of loopholes can be seen on the external and internal walls; another tier of fire was provided by merlons with loopholes, only a few of which survive.

The Ram Gate in Kumbhalgarh. The towers have a strong talus that is nearly vertical along most of its lower part and then abruptly comes to an end. This form of talus prevented the tower from being taken by escalade.

western one. The main entrance to Ranthambhor Castle, situated on its northern side, used to be barred with five gates, of which four survive.

The defences of plains castles, which generally have fewer gates at one entrance, were strengthened with barbicans and successive courtyards placed in various combinations. Several gates inside one entrance were usually connected by a winding passage or placed at 90 degrees to each other. Urban fortifications were given the fewest number of gates: their entrance was often no more than a gate with fortified outerwork.

Most entrances fall roughly into the following categories: first, a single gate was put across the road. This is the simplest possible design; it can be seen, for example, in the fortifications of the city and palace precincts of Tughluqabad, but is generally more characteristic of later fortifications of the 16th–18th centuries. The gate was usually strengthened with two flanking towers.

Second, a gate could be positioned beyond the projection of a wall. This is the structure of the first external gate (Naulakha Pol) at the northern entrance to the castle of Ranthambhor. A wall resembling a barbican was added in front of the gate and the passage between this and the internal wall was deliberately made too narrow for an elephant to turn round and attack the gate. The structure also protected the gate from projectiles from throwing machines.

Third, an external barbican might protect the gate. Structurally, this type closely resembles the previous one, but the outwork was more formidable. The barbican could have a curving, rectangular or semicircular shape. A curving barbican comprised two solid curtain walls brought forward and edged by towers. Both the walls and the towers were abundantly supplied with loopholes and machicolations, which would allow crossfire down onto an enemy in the narrow winding passage. This barbican usually had no gates on its outer side, but could have a drawbridge as, for example, in the Fateh Gate in Bidar. A barbican of this design is characteristic of urban fortifications. The inner gate on rectangular or semicircular barbicans was placed at 90 degrees to the outer one. The path leading from the entrance into the barbican towards the inner gate in the main wall usually made a turn to the left and very seldom to the right. (Similar passages in European fortifications usually bent right, as it forced the enemy to expose their right, unshielded side to the fire.) In general this type of barbican is characteristic of 16th–17th-century fortifications, though there are a few in Indian medieval castles. A semicircular barbican standing apart and in no way connected to the main wall can be seen in front of the Bala

The Fateh Gate – the principal entrance into the lower town of Bidar. The gate was reached by a winding passage flanked at the entrance by two formidable octagonal towers with box machicolations. There also used to be a drawbridge in front of these towers.

Hisar Gate in Golconda. The barbican has no gate and can be entered on the right as well as on the left. It seems to have been mainly designed for protecting the entrance to the citadel against attacks by elephants or siege engines.

Fourth, a complicated outer barbican with several gates and courts could protect a castle entrance. A combination of a semicircular barbican and two successive courts in front of the main gate can be seen at the entrance to the second line of defence in Daulatabad, the western gate of the citadel in Warangal, and the gate in the outer wall in Gingee. Entrances to the courts are protected with gates, and the passage between the gates makes several turns and constantly changes its direction.

Fifth, mountain castles or those standing on high hills, such as Chittorgarh, Ranthambhor or Gwalior, had multiple gates placed along a winding road. The gates are connected by curtain walls and were designed to command both straight sections of the road and its bends. On this fortified road a potential enemy would find themselves in the middle of a crossfire from the different levels of walls and gates. The gates along a serpentine road were generally simple: put across the road and flanked with towers. Only the extreme exterior and extreme interior gates were occasionally additionally fortified. There were exceptions, however. Toran Pol, or the fourth gate from the foot of the hill at the north entrance to Ranthambhor Castle, stands in a narrow place and overlooks the bedrock of the castle. Because of the layout, the gate could only be detected when the assailants were quite close to it. There is only a narrow strip of land between the gate and the rock where one had to make a turn at 90 degrees to enter the gate. It was too narrow to swing a battering ram, and an elephant could only turn with difficulty, so there was no question of attacking the gate at high speed. Moreover, the whole ground is exposed to fire on three sides: from the front, the side and the rear. This was undoubtedly the least accessible gate in Ranthambhor Castle.

The passage inside the gate itself was mostly straight, which certainly eased the task of those in attack. More complicated and safe was the passage where the path between the outer and inner gates made a turn at close to 90 degrees. This was designed to protect the inner gate from a high-speed elephant attack. The fifth gate (Andheri Pol) at the northern entrance to Ranthambhor Castle is an example of this kind of structure. The design was not very common, probably because it required a great gatehouse over the gate, which was uncharacteristic of Indian military architecture.

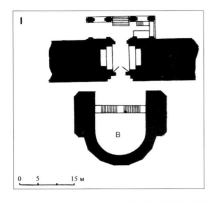

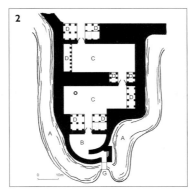

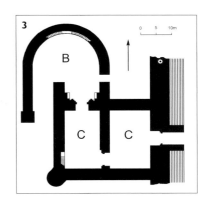

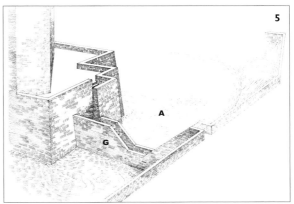

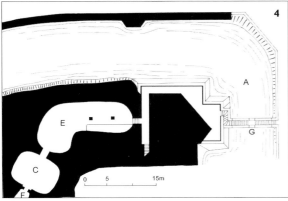

Behind the gate or along the sides of the gateway, accommodation was provided for the guards. Usually it was a little hall with columns supporting its roof. In Chittorgarh, there was another room for the guards situated in front of the seventh, inner gate (Ram Pol). This gate is at the uppermost end of the serpentine road, and the guards were probably on duty here to keep an eye on the entire length of the ascending road.

Although the gates described above are the most common styles, there are a number of other variations. The Mandu Gate in Bidar is marked by a unique structure: in front of it is a barbican filled with earth. The barbican's outer gate is built on ground level and a winding underground tunnel leads out on to the upper ground of the barbican to its inner gate. A well dug in the centre of the barbican allowed defenders to shoot down upon the enemy clambering upward. Moreover, halfway up the barbican there is a gallery supplied with loopholes on its outer side and arches on its inner side that give onto the well. The gallery commands the approaches to the outer gate as well as the enemy's movement up the underground tunnel. Even at the very top of the barbican, in front of the inner gate, the assailants would be exposed to crossfire from the main walls and towers.

The entrance to the citadel of Daulatabad is also well protected. The road here runs first along three sides of the tower, then over a cavern, across an open court and at last through a tunnel closed at the head by an iron shutter that moves horizontally on small wheels. The most curious thing is that the tunnel could be filled with a suffocating gas. For this purpose, a small room was built which opened onto the tunnel, and an iron brazier was kept there. About halfway along the tunnel an opening was made to create a draught, which could blow poisonous gas from the room to fill the tunnel. The method of smoking out an enemy had been known in Europe since ancient times, although it was only used here as a special measure against sappers in an underground tunnel.

ALL The layout of gates (after S. Toy): (1) Bala Hisar Gate, Golconda; (2) the gate in the outer wall, Gingee; (3) the West Gate leading to the citadel, Warangal; (4) entrance to the citadel, Daulatabad; (5) the bridge over the moat at the entrance to the citadel of Daulatabad. (A) moat; (B) barbican; (C) open court; (D) guardroom; (E) cavern; (F) tunnel; (G) bridge or drawbridge.

The inner, fifth gate (Andheri Pol) of the northern gate complex of Ranthambhor Castle. It is now partly destroyed, but the gateway used to pass through this gate along a dark tunnel, which made a turn to the right.

The most famous occasion on which it was used is the siege of Ambracia in 189 BC when the Greek defenders filled the underground gallery with an acrid gas and smoked out the Romans. In Daulatabad Castle the use of this method had been foreseen by the builders from the very beginning, which is a fine example of engineering ingenuity in fortification.

Gates themselves were usually double leaved, with a small door in one of the leaves. Unlike gateways, which were often made in the shape of an arch, the gate leaves were mostly rectangular and only rarely semi-arched. The small door was usually made in the left-hand leaf when looked at from the outside. A door in the right-hand shutter is much rarer. Doors were about 0.9m wide and 1.2m high. The leaves, up to 15cm thick, were made from hard, solid teak. They were strengthened by horizontal beams from behind and by iron plates at the front. They hung on heavy pivots fixed into stone sockets at the top and at the bottom. Gates were locked with a strong wooden bar that came out of an opening in the wall at one end and slid into an opening at the other end.

The width of gates varied from 3.6 to 4.8m, which is approximately the same as in European cities and castles, while the height exceeded the average figure for Europe and reached up to 7.5m. The height was governed by the fact

The Ganesh Gate is the fourth gate from the bottom in the north-east gate complex of Gwalior Castle. Built in the mid-15th century, it is an example of simple, unrefined Hindu architecture.

that the gateway had to be high enough for an elephant with a howdah on its back to pass through easily. This, however, made the gate vulnerable to attack by elephants, which were used by the Indians as live battering rams. Therefore, the outer surface of the leaves was stuck with thick, sharp iron or teak spikes. Nearly all the gates were fitted with spikes but not all of them have survived.

Spikes usually had a conical or polyhedral shape. Leaf-shaped spikes like those seen in Daulatabad Castle, or spikes with a hook, as in Kumbhalgarh and Chittorgarh, were comparatively rare. Spikes were sometimes decorated with petals branching off from the spike. The petals could lie parallel to the surface of the gate or spread in the same direction as the spikes, resembling a lily. Gulbarga Castle boasts unique spikes, each being a combination of four spirally twisted endings of equal length.

On some gates the spikes could cover the entire outer surface of the leaves; on others, they began at 1.5–2.4m above the ground and went up to the top; on still others, they covered only the part of the gate that was at the level of an elephant's forehead. The spikes were arranged in horizontal rows, eight to 15 spikes in a row, each 10 to 30cm apart. The length of the spikes varied from 7.5 to 33cm. To fasten

A comparatively rare type of anti-elephant spike with hooks can be seen on this gate of Kumbhalgarh. The spikes only cover a small part of the gate on a level with an elephant's forehead.

The central part of the tower at the fourth gate (Ganesh Pol) of the western gate complex of Chittorgarh. A unique construction device was used here: halfway up its height the tower is girdled with merlons. The merlons are false – no crenels of full value are to be found between them – but there are very real loopholes in the merlons themselves and in between. The shape of the merlons is also uncommon as they resemble buds.

the spike to the gate, its tang was run through the leaf and a horizontal wooden beam on its back, and turned down or riveted on a rectangular iron washer. As additional protection against the elephants, a heavy iron chain was sometimes stretched across the gateway.

A drawbridge sometimes fronted a gate, although they are not common in India. Meanwhile, a unique structure, a functional substitute for a drawbridge, can be seen in Daulatabad. A stationary bridge over a wide and deep water-filled moat connects the citadel to the road. The central part of the bridge lies lower than its ends and in time of attack the water level in the moat was raised by means of sluices and this part of the bridge was flooded.

Merlons, loopholes and machicolations

Most castle walls were edged with a parapet that protected a wall-walk along the top. A parapet usually consisted of merlons, (the solid part of the wall) and crenels (the indentations), which were considerably narrower than in European

A double wall in the north-west part of the upper town in Bidar. The external wall rises right from the bottom of the ditch; there is no berm. The merlons here have a rare three-lobed shape.

Loopholes and merlons of the barbican tower at the citadel gate in Tughluqabad seen from the inside. The direction of loopholes in the lower row alternates between looking downward and looking ahead. Each merlon in the parapet has three loopholes; the upper two are directed straight out and the lower one downward.

fortifications. Occasionally, a parapet was completely solid as, for example, the outer wall of Tughluqabad. There were also parapets provided with fake merlons. For example, at Chittorgarh the outer side of the solid parapet is covered with merlons carved in relief, which hides the fact that there are no real intervals between them.

As a rule, merlons have a semicircular, slightly sharpened flame-like shape in the upper half. This shape became widespread under Muslim influence and was probably first used in the fortifications of Siri, the second city of Delhi. Some merlons that can be seen at Chittorgarh are bud-like, or have the shape of an upside-down teardrop; others, for example in one section of the wall at Bidar, have a lobe-shaped upper part, but none of these was so common as flame-shaped merlons.

Crenels were often divided with one, two or three horizontal stone partitions into several narrow loopholes. There are some sectors in Golconda, for example, the Bala Hisar Gate and some parts of city walls and towers, where the crenels are completely covered with stone gratings.

Various types of merlons, loopholes, box machicolations and anti-elephant spikes

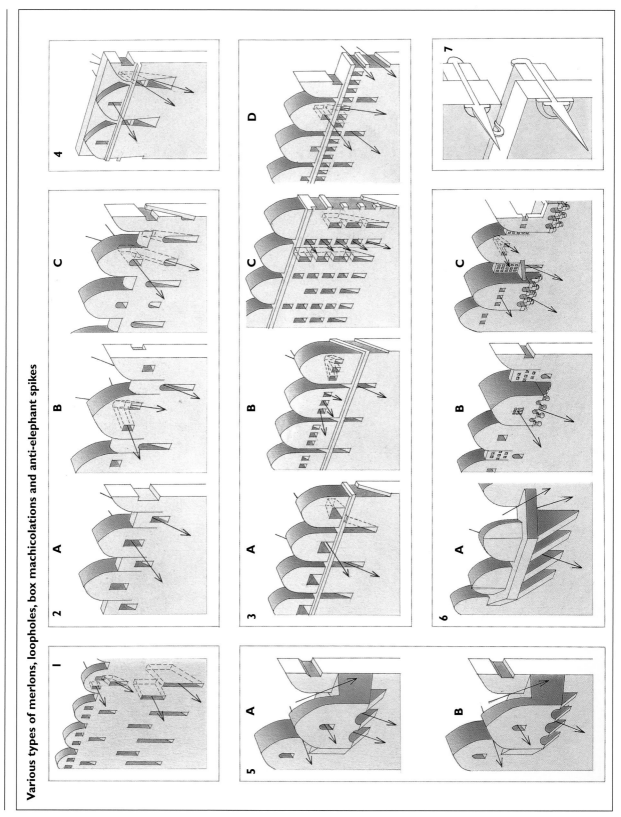

Various types of merlons, loopholes, box machicolations and anti-elephant spikes

Many Indian fortifications have parapets with peculiarly shaped merlons and complicated systems of loopholes, which differ substantially from similar structures in other countries. Typical Indian merlons were semicircular and pointed at the top, although they were sometimes fake: the parapet may be solid and the merlons shown in relief on the outside (as at Chittorgarh). What was unique is the arrangement and direction of loopholes. Loopholes were made both in the merlons themselves, and under the crenels. They could either look forward (to command distant approaches) or downward (to command the foot of the wall). Sometimes a merlon was pierced with two or three loopholes, but more often, one loophole was divided into two or three slits by horizontal or vertical partitions. The shape of loopholes, as well as the shape of merlons, need not have been the same everywhere in the castle, as shown by Kumbhalgarh. This picture shows various parapets: in Tughluqabad (**1**), Bidar (**2a–2c**), Kumbhalgarh (**3a–3d**) and Chittorgarh (**4**).

Box machicolations, characteristic of the Deccan fortification, are represented by those of Bidar (**5a–5b**) and Golconda (**6a** – earlier version on the citadel walls; **6b** – on the city walls; **6c** – on the barbican at the Bala Hisar Gate). For protection against an assault by elephants, the gates of Indian castles were generously studded with spikes (**7**). In order to fix a spike its tang was let through a gate leaf and a batten on the inner side, then bent or riveted.

In most fortifications a parapet was built with two tiers of loopholes, one formed by loopholes in the merlons of the parapet, and the other by slot machicolations directed downward from the wall-walk and emerging immediately under the parapet. If the wall had a mural gallery, it could also be provided with two tiers of loopholes – straight ones aimed at the horizon, and slot machicolations facing downward. This design can be seen on the walls of the fortified tomb of Ghiyath-ud-din Tughluq where there are four tiers of fire including the parapet. The walls of Tughluqabad had five tiers of fire: the inner and outer walls each had two tiers of loopholes in the parapet, and an extra one formed by the loopholes of the mural gallery in the inner wall.

Loopholes in this period were mostly just narrow vertical slits designed for archers. Crosslet slit loopholes were extremely rare, and the author has only found them in Kumbhalgarh. Crossbows were rarely used in medieval Indian armies so they were unnecessary. Loopholes with oillets (circular openings) at either end or at the centre of a vertical slit are never seen in Indian fortifications.

Loopholes varied greatly in size. They were about 10cm wide and about 90cm high in Chittorgarh, while in Tughluqabad they were 10 to 15cm wide and usually 30 to 45cm high, although the height of the lower loopholes in the outer wall sometimes reached 180cm.

BELOW The first part of the Triple Gate connecting the lower and upper towns in Bidar. This gate was built in a semicircular barbican that houses the second gate at its exit. In front of the barbican and the outer gate there was a moat, which was later filled in. The drawbridge over the moat does not survive either. Box machicolations, so characteristic of the Deccan fortification, are put not only above the gate but also along the barbican, protecting the foot of the wall and the 'dead ground' at wall bends.

There is immense variety in the arrangement and direction of loopholes: they were made in both the merlons themselves and in between. Some of them, intended for long-range fire, were directed straight out; others, meant for firing down onto the base of a wall, faced downward. Loopholes could widen outward or inward, occasionally affecting the shape of merlons: widened-slot machicolations at Chittorgarh, for example, give the merlons the shape of an upside-down teardrop. Some of the merlons are cut through with two to four loopholes arranged horizontally, vertically or in rows. The number of openings was then smaller on the inside than on the outside as one and the same loophole was simply separated in the thickness of the wall into several loopholes by horizontal or vertical divisions. In this case one of the openings of a loophole was directed straight out and the others sideward or downward. This greatly increased firepower in each direction and eliminated dead ground even at the foot of a wall. The shape and direction of loopholes was not necessarily the same for all the defences of a particular fortress and depended on the role of each sector in defence of the castle. A great variety of loopholes are represented in the walls of Kumbhalgarh.

Box machicolations (openings in the floor of the parapet) were popular in the castles of the Deccan. Placed above a gateway, at the approaches to a gate, above a ditch, or just along a wall, not only did they command the foot of the wall but they also allowed enfilade fire to be brought to bear

A machicolation in the wall at the Triple Gate in Bidar seen from the inside. Fire could be directed through it right ahead and sideward, as well as down at the ditch.
A rectangular loophole with a triangular upper part was designed for handguns. Such loopholes, along with rectangular ones with a rounded upper part, as well as strictly rectangular ones, can be seen in different sections of the walls at Bidar.

along the walls. Some of them were additionally provided with loopholes for frontal fire. Box machicolations were often open from the top and made at parapet level, as in Bidar and Golconda; they were just one or several merlons projecting from the wall line. Box machicolations covered on top and built below parapet level are considerably less common. In any case, they are generally placed on three or four corbels divided by two or three vertical openings respectively. A stone beam running from the wall to the outermost corbels would be erected either perpendicularly or at an angle. In the latter case, two more loopholes were sometimes added on the corners of the box machicolation. Longer machicolations lying on more than four corbels are less frequent and are generally only found above gates.

A tour of three castles

Three of the most famous castles are explored in detail in this section. They are situated in very different terrain and were constructed under the influence of a variety of architectural traditions. The Muslim rulers of the Delhi Sultanate built Tughluqabad, the third city of Delhi. The Bahmanids, the Muslim rulers of the Deccan, constructed Bidar according to the architectural conventions of the Deccan. Chittorgarh, built in Rajasthan (western India) by the Rajput rulers of Mewar, is an example of Hindu military architecture. All three fortresses were capitals of a state or a principality, and their fortifications were noted for their strength. Tughluqabad and Bidar are plain fortresses while Chittorgarh is a hill castle.

Tughluqabad

Tughluqabad was built by Ghiyath-ud-din Tughluq in 1321–25. It occupies a vast area and consists of the city, the palace precincts and the citadel. The walls stretch for nearly 6.5km, conforming to the contours of a rocky outcrop. A moat was dug out on all sides except the south where a depression fronting the walls became a lake in the rainy season.

The walls of Tughluqabad are quite well preserved and, though lacking most of the parapet, remain impressively strong. At the foot of the walls is a rocky outcrop faced with masonry, which makes the walls look much higher on the outside than on the inside. The height of the walls round the city and the palace precincts reaches from 10 to 15m on the outside. The inner walls dividing the three enclosures are approximately the same height. As for the citadel walls, some sections on the outside are nearly 30m above the valley.

The rubble-built walls were faced with ashlar, which was readily pilfered by the local population after the city was abandoned, and in many places the rubble core is visible.

Strong towers are positioned every 50 to 100m; most are semicircular, but some are circular or rectangular. The towers protrude beyond the curtain wall, allowing effective enfilade fire. These towers are as high as the castle walls, which is common in Indian fortifications, and taper upward in a cone shape. The Tughluqabad fortifications are characterized by a solid talus, which is manifestly bigger on the towers than on the curtain walls.

The dilapidated walls of Tughluqabad. The facing has fallen down in places, uncovering a rubble core.

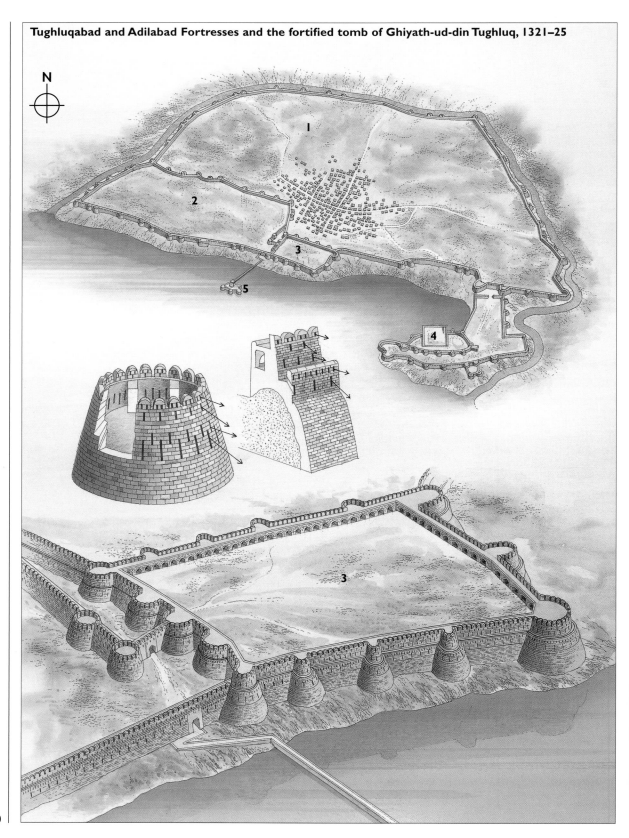

Tughluqabad or the third city of Delhi, was built by Ghiyath-ud-din Tughluq and consists of the city (**1**), the palace precincts (**2**) and the citadel (**3**). Ghiyath-ud-din Tughluq's son and successor Muhammad bin Tughluq supplemented Tughluqabad, on its southern extremity, with a moderate-sized fortress, Adilabad (**4**), which in its turn consists of a citadel and an outer ward. A causeway connects Tughluqabad with the fortified tomb of Ghiyath-ud-din Tughluq (**5**). The season of rains used to turn this fortified tomb into an islet in the middle of a lake. The drawing shows a reconstruction of the citadel of Tughluqabad (**3**). A barbican in front of the gate connecting the citadel with the palace precincts can be seen in the foreground.

Tughluqabad has double walls. A second, lower wall stands only 1.5 to 2m apart from the interior one. A solid, unbroken parapet with two rows of loopholes runs along this outer wall. The upper loopholes look out to the distance, while those at the bottom of the parapet command the foot of the wall. The inner wall has a row of short loopholes just above the parapet level of the outer wall. They correspond to a mural gallery. In addition, the inner wall has a battlemented parapet pierced with two more tiers of fire: one through the crenels and loopholes in the merlons, and the other through the loopholes at the bottom of the parapet, directed downward. All in all, there were five tiers of fire in this double wall.

The city walls are pierced with numerous gates. There are two more gates in the outer walls of the palace precincts and another two in the inner walls connecting the city and the palace precincts. The citadel has no gates in its outer walls. Only a hidden underground postern provides for an escape in the last resort. However strong, gates were always the weak spots in defences. A gate leading into the citadel was only built on the side of the palace precincts. An enemy was forced to seize this area before they could reach the citadel gate, which was protected by a barbican with strong towers. The barbican gate can only be approached along the citadel wall. Here, the assailants would find themselves under fire from the right-hand, less protected side. The inner gate is placed at 90 degrees to the outer one.

In 1325 Muhammad bin Tughluq, son and successor of Ghiyath-ud-din Tughluq, added a moderate-sized fortress called Adilabad on the southern side of Tughluqabad. It was also known as Muhammadabad, after the sultan. The fortress consists of a citadel and an outer ward and the walls of Adilabad resemble those of Tughluqabad in structure. As in Tughluqabad, there is an arched mural gallery with loopholes. A wall-walk with a battlemented parapet runs above the gallery. A causeway connected Tughluqabad and Adilabad, and sluices allowed control of the water level in the lake, as well as irrigation of the neighbouring fields. Adilabad was supplied with several gates, some of them with a barbican in front. One gate is particularly curious. Halfway down the passage its vaulted gateway turns to the left at a right angle. There were two double-leaved doors at the entrance and exit of the gateway and rooms for the guards on either side of it.

Another interesting structure, the tomb of Ghiyath-ud-din Tughluq, adjoins Tughluqabad on the south-west. The tomb is connected to the

BELOW Loopholes in the external wall of Tughluqabad. The upper loopholes were designed for long-range fire, while the lower ones commanded the area at the base of the wall.

The tomb of Ghiyath-ud-din Tughluq. A causeway connects this little fortress with Tughluqabad. The fortress used to be washed by the waters of a lake.

southern gate of the palace precincts by a causeway; it was once a small island in the middle of a lake. It is a small-sized fortress with strong walls and five towers. The structure and the style of its fortifications are the same as those of Tughluqabad, but it has no outer wall and there are four tiers of fire – two in the mural gallery and two at parapet level. The tomb was built *c.*1325 and Ghiyath-ud-din Tughluq, his wife and son Muhammad bin Tughluq lie here. A store chamber and a well suggest that a permanent garrison was billeted here. The tomb was a self-sufficient section of the defence system, able to withstand a siege.

Bidar

Most of the fortifications at Bidar date from 1429–32, although the parapet of the wall was rebuilt in the 16th–17th centuries to strengthen the defences against the firepower of handguns. Behind the walls three circular tower pedestals, named Black, Red and Long, were erected for mounting heavy cannon. Some of the gates were rebuilt, too, and the dates of the rebuild can be seen on the first and second of the Triple Gate – 1683 and 1503 respectively.

The fortifications of Bidar in the north-west part of the upper town, viewed from the Delhi Gate. Here, the fortifications consist of a double wall and ditch. The citadel on the hill is visible in the distance.

A view, through a crenel, of the walls of Bidar in the neighbourhood of the Triple Gate. Projecting far beyond the wall level, the towers allowed effective flanking fire and command of the entire length of the moat. This was further assisted by box machicolations, which often looked like a merlon projecting beyond the wall line.

The fortifications of Bidar consist of the lower town, the upper town and the citadel. The upper town, especially the citadel, stand on a height. The citadel is in the northern corner of the upper town and adjoins the town's fortifications on two sides, forming two lines of defence. Walls on the side of the upper town also protected the citadel, but they are in poor condition now.

The fortifications of the upper town are fairly well preserved and very impressive. The thickness of the walls varies from 5 to 15m. The towers along the walls are circular or octahedral, sometimes square. Many are squat. The western and southern sides boast the strongest fortifications. Here the walls are thickest, and a triple moat runs before them; tower-pedestals for cannon are here, too. In the north-west section there is a double wall and a ditch between the Delhi Gate and the citadel. The defences of the eastern side are confined to a single high wall as the steep slopes of the hill offer natural defensive advantages.

Many gates break up the walls of Bidar: two in the citadel, six in the upper town and five in the lower town. One of the citadel gates led into the upper town, the other to an open space beyond the walls, from where an escape could be made if the town fell. All six gates of the upper town are unique in their structure, but the Triple and Mandu Gates are especially interesting. The Triple Gate connects the upper town with the lower one, and its fortifications are particularly strong. On the right and left of the gate's barbican complex runs a triple moat partitioned at the ends and in the middle with sluices that could flood the ditches in case of danger. This construction, in combination with moats cut in rocky soil, was a unique engineering decision. The moats are about 9m deep; the two outer sections are about 10.5m wide, and inner one is 13m wide. On the western side the triple moat runs on beyond its junction with the walls of the lower town; on the eastern side it ends where the walls of the lower and upper towns meet. Here, at the end of the central moat, a solid squat tower guards this vulnerable spot. Low walls probably ran along the top of the longitudinal partitions left after digging the moats; together with the main wall, they formed several lines of defence. At least one section of similar walls can be seen to the east of the Triple Gate. A low wall also ran on the outside of the moats, although nothing but its foundation survives.

The Triple Gate, as its name suggests, is made up of three successive gates. The first, outer gate is situated at the side of a semicircular barbican, which has strong walls crowned with box machicolations. While approaching this gate, the enemy's unprotected right-hand side would be exposed to fire from the walls of the upper town. In front of this gate there was a moat with a drawbridge, but neither survive. The Sharza Gate, so-called because of two tigers carved in relief above the gateway, is on the other side of the barbican. This gate is lavishly

Bidar Castle

The surviving fortifications mostly date back to 1429–32. Some rebuilding work was done in the 16th–17th centuries and was mainly concerned with the adaptation of the battlements to defence against firearms. The fortress consists of the lower city, the upper city and the citadel. The gates of the lower city resemble one another. They consist of a barbican, which has a winding passage running along the formidable walls with towers at each end. Here, an enemy is exposed to crossfire from loopholes and box machicolations. Shown in the drawing are two gates of the lower city: the Fateh (1) and Talghat (2) Gates. Each gate of the upper city is different and the Triple (3) and Mandu (4) Gates are the most interesting of them. The Triple Gate, which connects the lower and upper cities, consists of three successive gates. The first two are in a semicircular barbican; the second and third gates are connected by a long passage with low battlemented walls on either side, commanding the triple moat in front of the main wall of upper city. There was once a moat and drawbridge in front of the first gate, but it no longer exists. The structure of the Mandu Gate is quite unique. A barbican filled with earth is positioned in front of the gate, and a winding underground tunnel leads from the outer gate in the barbican to the top of the barbican. A well dug in the centre of the barbican allows fire to be brought to bear upon the enemy climbing upward. Moreover, halfway up the barbican there is a gallery supplied with loopholes on its outer side and arches on its inner side that give onto the well. But even if assailants succeeded in getting to the inner gate at the very top of the barbican, they would find themselves under fire on three sides: from the front, from the side and from behind.

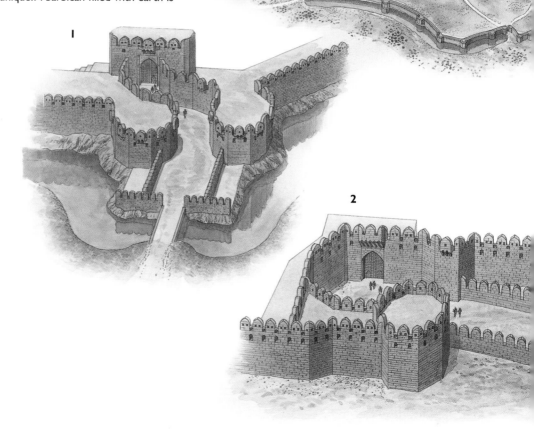

Lower city

1

2

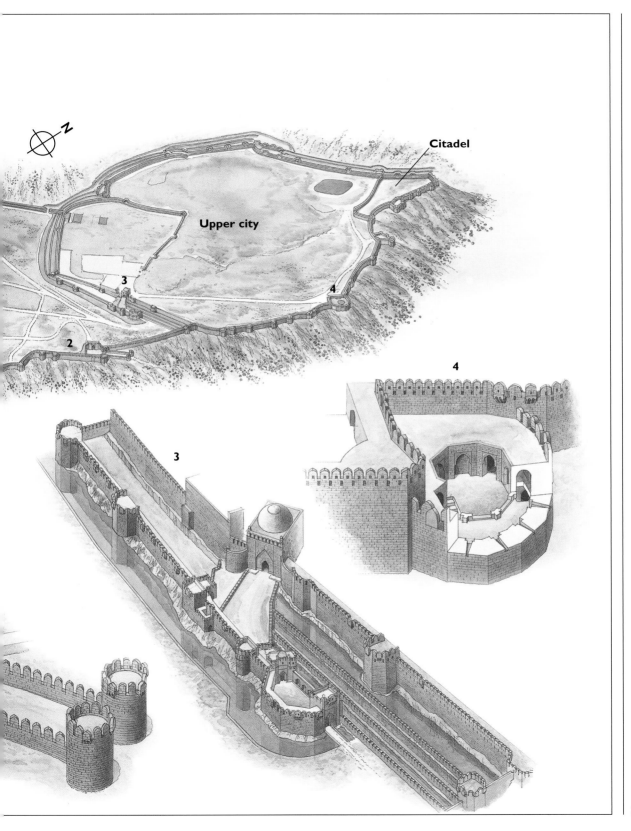

Citadel

Upper city

3

4

2

3

4

A view of the triple moat from the fortified passage leading from the second to the third gate of the Triple Gate. Low walls with merlons fortify the passage, allowing flanking fire along all three ditches.

decorated with multicoloured mosaics and was beautiful; it is very impressive even now in spite of its peeling walls. The road from the second to the third gate lies across the moat and is strengthened by low battlemented walls on either side. A triple moat on its right-hand side is exposed to fire from the crenels of that wall. On the left there is an extended fortification, where the barbican walls, strengthened with towers, run parallel to the main wall for 200–250m before adjoining it. The third gate, the Gumbad Gate, is an excellent example of Muslim architecture. It has a dome, arched niches on either side, and the gateway itself widens inside the gate, forming a circular drum with eight arches, two of which are passageways and the rest are blind niches.

The Mandu Gate on the eastern side of the upper town, guarded by a barbican filled with earth and accessed by an underground tunnel, is described in more detail on page 21.

All five gates of the lower town (Fateh, Mangalpet, Dulhan, Shahganj and Talghat) are similar in many respects. They are protected at the front by a barbican, through which a passage leads to the gate. This path is narrow and winding, sometimes bending at a right angle, which would place an enemy under crossfire from the walls and towers. Numerous box and slot machicolations allowed concentrated fire upon the enemy, leaving no dead ground. Some barbicans consisted of two walls with strong towers at their ends (Fateh and Talghat Gates). Others, such as the Dulhan Gate, were protected by a barbican wall and tower positioned so that there was a passage between the barbican wall and the main wall of the fortress. It is interesting that the barbican here did not begin with a gate, but a drawbridge was built in front of some of the gates.

The parapet of the walls with its loopholes and box machicolations deserves special mention. The merlons have a characteristic semicircular shape pointing upward; they are about 0.9m thick and 2.2–2.6m high. Loopholes were made both in the merlons and under the crenels. Those under the crenels were directed downward and functioned as machicolations. The loopholes in the merlons faced several directions. Some loopholes had the familiar one opening on the outside and one on the inside. However, Bidar also boasts loopholes of a more complex design, with two openings on the outside corresponding to one on the inside. Such loopholes fork out inside the wall allowing fire in two directions, in horizontal or vertical planes. Box machicolations, so typical of the military architecture of the Deccan, are mostly positioned on the parapet level in Bidar and are represented by one merlon projecting beyond the line of the wall. Longer and more powerful machicolations, consisting of two or three merlons, can only be seen above a few gates.

The fortified passage to the Gumbad Gate in Bidar, the third (internal) gate of the Triple Gate dividing the upper town from the lower one. The Gumbad Gate has a domed roof; the gateway widens inside the gatehouse. There are eight arches here, only two of which are for passing through, the rest being 'blind'. This square gatehouse, with a dome and an arched thoroughfare, has all the characteristic features of Muslim architecture.

Chittorgarh

One of the most famous castles of Rajasthan, founded in AD 728, Chittorgarh belonged almost uninterruptedly to the rulers of Mewar, and was the capital of the principality until besieged by the Mughal emperor Akbar in 1567–68.

The castle crowns a flat narrow summit of a hill, towering 152m above the surrounding valley. The walls stretching along the edge of the hill are a continuation of its steep slopes; their lower part is the rock itself faced with stone. As a result, they look higher from the outside than from the inside, where their height is no more than 2–3m.

Most of the fortifications date from the 13th century and are an excellent example of Hindu military architecture. Having seized the castle, the Muslims rebuilt nothing but a few parts of the parapet and some of the gates.

The main entrance is on the western side where seven gates are set up along a winding road. The first gate up the hill (Padal Pol) is the oldest, dating from c.1100. Its lower part is built of large hewn stones, roughly coursed, and the parapet of smaller but well-coursed stones. It is interesting that the gate is flanked by a full-sized tower on the left and only a small fragment of one on the right. The builders probably thought it unnecessary to erect a full-sized tower on the side where a long curtain wall adjoins the gate. The loopholes in the curtain commanded the approaches to the gate where an enemy would have exposed their right, unshielded side to flanking fire. The second gate (Bhairon Pol) is famous because here in 1568 Emperor Akbar fired a bullet that killed Jaimal, leader of the defence. The place of his death is marked near the gate, while the gate itself only attracts attention because of the fresh paint and recent restoration work. This cannot be said about the third gate (Hanuman Pol), which preserves its original appearance and is an excellent example of Hindu architecture. Unfortunately, the upper part of the fourth gate (Ganesh Pol) does not survive. However, the only tower standing by the gate at the turn of the road deserves special attention. This circular tower is unique in having false merlons with

The Delhi Gate in Bidar. The external gate sits in the barbican. The gate is protected with box machicolations from above and one side. In order to get from the external to the internal gate one has to go through the barbican and turn left at 90 degrees.

Chittor Castle

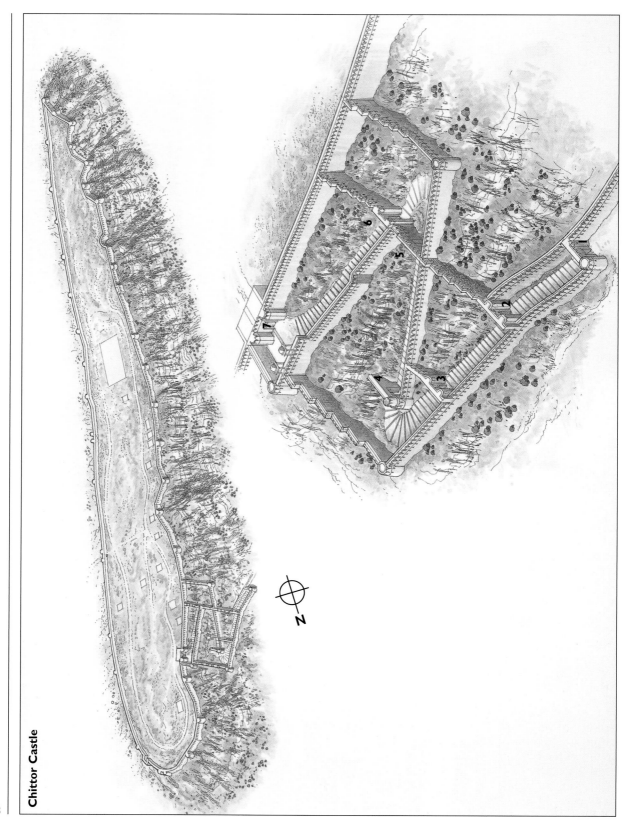

Most of the fortifications of the castle date from the 13th century, although examples of earlier fortifications from the 11th–15th centuries are also to be found here; some elements, such as large square embrasures for cannon were added even later. The castle has three entrances of which the western entrance shown in the inset is of particular interest. Here, an ascending winding road is provided with seven gates: Padal Pol (**1**), Bhairon Pol (**2**), Hanuman Pol (**3**), Ganesh Pol (**4**), Jorla Pol (**5**), Lakshman Pol (**6**) and Ram Pol (**7**). This gate complex is protected both by longitudinal walls along the road, and transversal walls which prevented an enemy from bypassing any of the gates. An enemy ascending the road would be exposed to fire from several tiers of the walls, and from the towers beside the gates.

loopholes placed halfway up the wall. The merlons are unusual in shape: divided into three segments, they resemble a bud. The fifth gate is called Jorla Pol or Joined Gate, because the upper part adjoins the foot of the sixth gate. The arch on the fifth gate is the legacy of Muslim rulers who rebuilt it. The heads of the passages on the other gates of the western entrance have lintels and corbels characteristic of Hindu architecture, but Jorla Pol was rebuilt and received the pointed arch typical of Muslim architecture.

Past the monumental sixth gate (Lakshman Pol) the road turns slightly and leads to the most beautiful seventh gate (Ram Pol). The gate and two octagonal towers flanking it were built in 1459 from large, finely dressed stones; they were lavishly decorated with relief, ornamental edgings and projections. Unfortunately, the upper part of the structure has been destroyed. The original overlap, decorated with relief carvings, probably lies in front of the gate near the hall of the guard, directly opposite Ram Pol. The hall of the guard was built in Hindu style and is composed of multiple columns covered with relief. Two small pavilions, or *chatri*, are undoubtedly a later addition. Directly behind the gate, on either side of the passage, there were two more colonnaded rooms for the guard; they now lie in ruins.

The walls of the gate complex have many loopholes, which ensured a multi-tier defence. The enemy on the road was exposed to fire from the upper tiers of the wall and from the gate, which overlooks the bends and the straight parts of the road. To prevent the besiegers avoiding any section of the road and rounding the defenders' flank, cross-walls were erected which snake up the hill in ledges. Apart from this primary function, the cross-walls allowed the defence to conduct flanking fire all along the main walls of the castle.

Besides the western gate complex there were two more entrances to the castle. The eastern entrance has four gates, the uppermost of which is called Suraj Pol or Sun Gate. The northern entrance is only defended by one gate placed at the end of a precipitous path. On the southern extremity there is a small opening right in the wall; it was specially designed for throwing criminals and traitors down onto the rocks below.

The parapet of the wall and the shape of the merlons and loopholes are noteworthy. All the merlons are false and can only be seen from the outside, while on the inside the parapet is solid, without crenels. There are two main shapes of merlons in Chittorgarh: straight and vertical, or an upside-down teardrop. The first are comparatively rare: they can be seen on the second (Bhairon Pol) and the fifth (Jorla Pol) gates of the western gate complex, for example. The second are everywhere, although the size and form of the drop varies from one curtain wall to another. On some walls, their bottom (or the top of the drop) is stretched out

The first gate from the bottom (Padal Pol) of the western gate complex in Chittorgarh. The gate was built c.1100 and is an excellent example of early Hindu architecture. The lower part of the gate was laid with large hewn stones, roughly coursed, and the parapet with false merlons – of smaller but well-coursed stones.

and pointed at the end; on others it is wide as if it were clipped. The size of the merlons varies respectively from about 1.5 to 3m. The upper part of the drops on the fourth gate (Ganesh Pol) is further divided into three segments and resembles a bud. Despite these differences, however, all the merlons of Chittorgarh are semicircular, tapering to a point at the top.

Loopholes mostly alternate: straight ones, for long-range fire, are in the middle of the merlons, while those for shooting downwards are between them. Hence in a drop-shaped merlon, the loophole for firing downwards is substantially widened out, forming a bell-bottom, and the longer the foot of the merlon, the greater the fire angle. On the inside of the walls loopholes directed downward are narrow vertical slits, while those for long-range fire widen sideways. There is a narrow belt along the middle of the merlons which divides straight loopholes from downward loopholes. Moreover, some loopholes are divided by one or two additional horizontal partitions. Large square embrasures in the middle of the merlons on some sections of the walls were designed for cannon and were added later.

Immediately next to the western entrance of the castle is the wall of Banbeer, which was built in a hurry directly opposite the Palace of Rana Kumbha during the siege of Chittorgarh by the Sultan of Gujarat in 1534–35. Banbeer, who had usurped the throne, decided to erect the wall to divide the castle of Chittor into two parts. For lack of stone, the builders used stone from various buildings, including columns and relief-embossed slabs. However, the castle fell and the wall remained unfinished.

Interiors and living quarters

Most Indian castles have a citadel. Citadels of the ancient Harappan civilization were positioned outside a city, but in medieval times they were usually to be found inside urban fortifications, generally on a hillock. They were often positioned in one corner of a city (rather than the middle) so that the urban defences doubled as the external fortifications of the citadel. In Golconda the citadel stands on a hill almost in the centre, while the citadels of Bidar and Tughluqabad are placed on the least accessible sides of the city. The appearance of a citadel within the borders of Indian cities is sometimes explained by Greek influence (the campaign of Alexander the Great or the Greeks of Bactria), or influence from the Crusaders transferred via the Muslims. However, neither explanation is correct. Describing Alexander's campaign, the Greek historian Arrian (VI.7.4–6; VI.9.1–VI.11.1) mentions citadels where Indians hid themselves during an attack, having failed to hold the urban fortification. This proves that citadels were characteristic of Indian cities before Alexander the Great invaded them.

Donjons, which were commonplace in European castles, were practically never built in India. The only exception is Bala Hissar in Gulbarga Castle. This small, rectangular structure with circular towers, battlemented walls and a stone staircase leading to a considerably elevated entrance, could be described as a donjon or a very small citadel.

The *Shilpashastras* mention four types of structures: palaces of the nobility (*raja-bhavana*), temples (*deva-bhavana*), common people's dwelling houses (*jana-bhavana*) and public buildings (recreation centres, libraries, water reservoirs, wells and so on). Palaces and temples were certainly the most important buildings and were constructed with special thoroughness and care – as a rule, they are generally the best preserved.

When the Muslim conquerors came to power in northern India and later in the Deccan, the appearance of castles and cities changed considerably. Temples were destroyed and mosques erected in their place. In Delhi alone, 27 Hindu and Jaina temples were demolished, and their materials used in the construction of the Quwwat-ul-Islam ('Might of Islam') mosque. Another monumental architectural structure to become quite common from the time of the Delhi sultans was a ruler's tomb. A tomb usually occupied a spacious, fenced site, was lavishly decorated and represented a real masterpiece of architectural art, though these tombs were far inferior to those of their Mughal successors. The earliest

A lavatory in Indian castles, like in medieval European castles, was just a small closet overhanging a wall. All human waste fell down onto the walls of the castle or into the ditch. A lavatory on the castle wall in Ranthambhor can be seen in the centre of the left-hand photograph. the interior view is shown in the photograph on the right.

Man Mandir Palace. Built between 1486 and 1516 by Raja Man Singh, this palace is the most beautiful of the six palaces of Gwalior Castle and one of the most interesting examples of early Hindu platial architecture.

surviving structures of this type were the tombs of Iltutmish and the so-called 'Sultan Ghari', the latter built for the sultan's son. Some tombs were enclosed within a defensive wall and were really small fortresses. The tomb of Ghiyath-ud-din Tughluq, constructed close to Tughluqabad and connected to it by a causeway, is the most widely known of these fortified tombs.

The palace was the principal building inside a castle, whether of a Hindu or Muslim ruler. Kautilya (Art. II, 4 (22)) recommends positioning a king's palace a little to the north of the city centre. It should occupy one-ninth of the construction site, its front facing either east or north. Other canonical texts, however, advise that a palace be placed right in the centre of a fortress, undoubtedly for reasons of security. In reality, a palace was only built in the centre of a plain fortress; in case of a hill or mountain castle it would stand in the least accessible part of the precincts.

The central place in a palace was reserved for dwelling apartments (*dhavalgriha*), which were divided into men's (*mardana*) and women's (*zenana*) zones. No man could enter the female quarters except the ruler himself, eunuchs and aged courtiers. A separate palace for women, such as the Palace of Rani Padmini in Chittorgarh, was a rare exception. Besides apartments, a palace would house a kitchen, a bath complex, gardens, lakes, often with fountains, and halls of audiences.

Practically every Indian castle had a palace, often more than one. Chittorgarh had several, the three most famous being the Palace of Rana Kumbha, Padmini's Palace and the Palace of Rattan Singh II. The enclosed territory of the Palace of Rana Kumbha encompasses the main court with the ruler's private apartments, the inner court and three-storey women's apartments (*zenana*), the public audience hall and a complex of buildings presumably meant for the heirs. There were also other structures, such as elephant stables, a place for offering prayers to the sun, and a temple. A wall with only two gates – the Badi Pol and Tripolia – encircled the palace. Decorated with numerous balconies and ornamental bands and flower head bosses, it does not in any way resemble a severe-looking fortress. Gwalior Castle has six palaces. The most famous of them is the Man Mandir, often called the most beautiful palace in India. It comprises two courts surrounded by multiple premises – living rooms, colonnaded halls, dancing halls, pavilions, underground chambers (including those for torture), secret passages and so on. The palace facade is lavishly decorated with ornate fretwork and colourful insets.

The garrison lived in barracks or arched hollows in the walls. These niche-chambers can be seen in the walls of Tughluqabad and Adilabad. The gate guards occupied special rooms behind or on the sides of the gateway.

Castles would be stored with plentiful supplies of food and weapons in case of siege. Special storehouses were set aside for corn, oil, salt, dried vegetables, wood and so on. Castles covering a large area, such as Kumbhalgarh, for example, even encompassed arable lands near water reservoirs. These ensured complete self-sufficiency for the defenders and allowed them to withstand a siege of several years' duration.

Particular attention was paid to water supplies. Sometimes a natural spring was right in the territory of the castle, as in Gingee, Gwalior or Mandu. However, natural springs were not to be found everywhere and it was not safe to depend on one source of water, as the besiegers could block it. So each castle had a large tank for gathering rainwater during monsoons. Wells were less common. While it was not difficult to dig them out in a plains castle, it was practically impossible to reach down to the water level in a mountain one. In Kashmir, where it snows more often than it rains, they melted snow for drinking water.

Indian castles often housed a tank of water. It was used for ritual ablution, as a bathing place for the nobility and, finally, as a source of drinking water in case of siege. One such tank, protected by an additional external wall, can be seen off the main wall of Chittor Castle.

The castles in war

Pre-Muslim India remained backward in siege technology. Crude throwing machines are mentioned in ancient Indian texts such as *The Arthashastra*, but how widely these were used is still arguable. We know, however, that they were not widespread in the early Middle Ages. The Muslim conquerors brought a new vigour to siege warfare with their expertise in siege techniques.

In their aggressive campaigns the Delhi sultans made extensive and profitable use of the achievements of the Islamic world in siege warfare. They often used incendiaries and throwing machines, less frequently they used sapping. Movable siege towers were rarely, if ever, used. Cannon did not play any part in siege warfare and made no impact on fortification in the pre-Mughal period.

Stone-throwing machines (*manjaniqs*) are mentioned in several sieges at the castle of Ranthambhor in 1290–1301. During the first (1290–91), Jalal-ud-din Khalji tried to build raised platforms, probably planning to mount throwing machines on them, but the attempt failed. Ala-ud-din Khalji's army used throwing machines at the sieges of Ranthambhor (1300–01) and Chittorgarh (1303). In the early 14th century, in the Warangal campaign, Malik Kafur ordered that stone balls be gathered for the *manjaniq maghribi* that were positioned all around the encircled castle, so presumably the defenders also had throwing machines and threw stone balls at the besiegers. Throwing-machines are known to have been used by the defenders of Ranthambhor in 1300–01. At Siwana stones from *manjaniq maghribi* flew into the castle from all sides, which shows that the besiegers did not concentrate their throwing machines together in one battery, but placed them all along the perimeter.

Armies in India rarely used battering rams in the European sense of the word. They were used on a few occasions in the Middle Ages, but on the whole they were never popular. Indians preferred elephants to wooden battering rams, and they served as living rams from epic times to the end of the 18th century. Pushing forward with their foreheads and working with their tusks and forelegs, they were capable of destroying not only gates, but also masonry and brick walls. For protection against an elephant attack, the gate leaves of practically every castle were embedded with sharp spikes, but even this did not always help. An infuriated elephant, provoked into frenzy by fire and driven to the gate at high speed, would break it in spite of the spikes. The head and tusks of an attacking elephant were often protected with iron plates.

Elephants played a decisive part in the assault on the castle of Taq besieged by Mahmud of Ghazni in the course of one of his 17 raids on India in the early 11th century. According to one historian, Mahmud of Ghazni:

> Ordered the ditch to be filled in. The besiegers then crossed over in the face of a shower of stones and missiles and attacked the gates of the castle which crashed down under the furious charge of the elephants. The assailants rushed in to occupy the outer fortifications. The defenders fought bravely and contested every inch of the ground, but when Khalaf saw Mahmud's elephants trampling his men to death he was so disconcerted that he offered submission and surrendered the castle.[1]

In other sources Ibn Batutah tells us about mining at the time of Muhammad bin Tughluq. In 1472 Mahmud Gawan made successful use of mining at the siege of Belgaun Castle. The method of burning away props was practically the only one

---

[1] Nizam M., *The Life and Times of Sultan Mahmud of Ghazna* (New Delhi, 1971), pp. 68–69

Standing on top of a hill, the citadel of Kumbhalgarh is surrounded by several rings of walls and includes the 19th-century Badal Mahal or Cloud Palace. A winding road leads upward and is barred with a number of gates. Rana Kumbha built Kumbhalgarh's powerful defensive walls in 1443–58.

used in underground warfare until the 16th century when it was replaced by applying a powder charge.

In spite of the great variety of siege techniques, Indian castles were taken more often by bribery than blockade. Resorting to passive blockades was especially characteristic of Hindu rulers. These blockades often lasted for months on end. The siege laid by the Rajputs to the castle of Sarhind following their significant victory over Muhammad of Ghur in the first battle at Tarain (1191) lasted 13 months before the garrison capitulated. The siege of Akhan Lohana by Rai Chach lasted a year.

For a blockade to be successful it was necessary to surround the castle with a thick ring of besieging troops, allowing no reinforcement or food supplies into it. It was also advisable to block access to the sources of water or else to poison the supplies. Thirst made the besieged surrender sooner than hunger. Uninterrupted siege lines around a besieged castle, such as those built by the Romans under Julius Caesar, were not typical of India. Instead, the cordon generally consisted of military posts placed at regular intervals, with cavalry or infantry units moving in between. The following episode of the siege of Sirahshila (Kashmir) in 1144 gives an idea of how thick the ring around a castle could be:

> The royal troops kept them [the besieged] in excitement day and night by all possible means and blocked [their access to] the water by boats which were moving about … when he [Bhoja] was then preparing to start [escape] at night he saw from the tower of the castle that all [enemies] awake around about and in their camp the fires blazing. These lit up the castle so much so that even an ant could not have moved out by the main road without being noticed by the watchful enemies. This made it impossible for him to leave. Then, when the day broke out after that night, the Damara let him climb down the precipice fastened to a rope.[2]

Bhoja waited several days for an opportunity to slip unnoticed past the guard but at last, disappointed, climbed up some ropes and back into the castle.

Fortresses often fell because of treachery. When Muhammad Kasim besieged Multan in AD 713, the Hindus resisted until a deserter revealed the whereabouts of the spring that supplied the town with water. The Muslims blocked the spring and the garrison quickly surrendered. Having besieged the castle of Uch, Muhammad of Ghur (r.1173–1206) tried to tempt the raja's wife into becoming the principal wife of his harem. She declined this honour in favour of her daughter, caused her husband to be put to death and surrendered the castle.

---

[2] Kalhana's *Rajatarangini*, VII, 1181–91, VIII, 2541ff.

Ranthambhor Castle, 13th–15th centuries

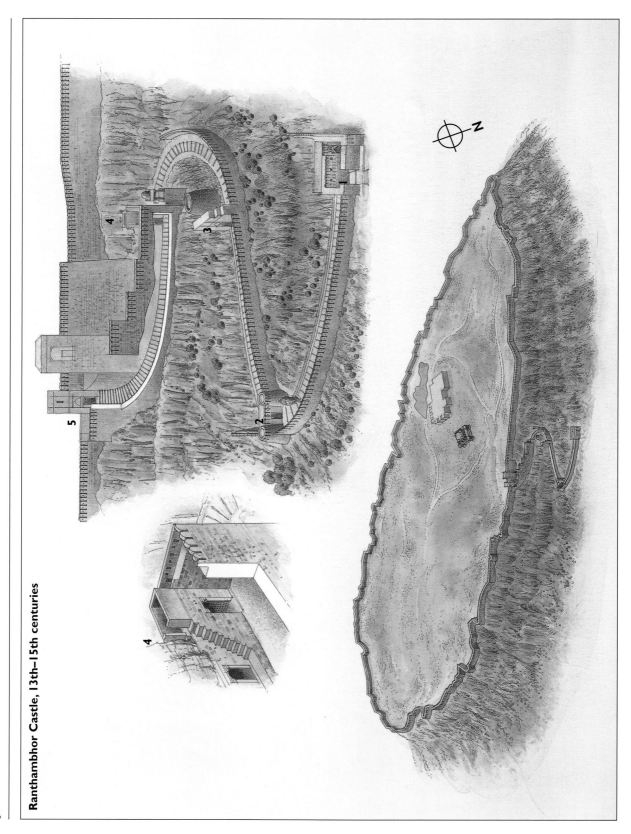

The castle was probably built in AD 944, but the fortifications that can be seen now mainly date from the 13th century, with some alterations from the 15th century and later. The main entrance to the castle is situated on the northern side where a complex of five gates was built along a winding road. The passage leading to the first gate (**1**, Naulakha Pol) is partitioned by an outer wall forming a kind of barbican; one can only reach the gate after making a sharp turn and passing along a narrow path running between the walls. This prevented an enemy from attacking the gate with an elephant. The second gate, (**2**, Hathi Pol) has not survived. Access to it was barred with a huge stone figure of an elephant with a drover sitting on it. The third gate (**3**, Ganesh Pol) is adorned with a sculptural image of Ganesh, the god of good luck and prosperity. The fourth gate (**4**, Toran Pol) is the most powerful of the five. It stands on the road right after a sharp turn and was not visible to the enemy until they came close up to it. It looks out onto a rock and one needs to make a 90-degree turn to the left to get into it. This construction prevented an enemy from attacking the gate with an elephant at high speed. A long tunnel that makes a turn to the right inside the gatehouse was a peculiarity of the fifth gate (**5**, Andheri Pol).

Stones were always popular defensive weapons. Light stones thrown by hand served as anti-personnel weapons, while heavy boulders rolled down walls were far more formidable. Flung from a high wall, particularly of a mountainous castle, they inflicted enormous casualties on the manpower of the assailants; they also damaged siege weapons, breaking scaling ladders and the roofs of wooden covers. Rallied by Bhikshu, the defenders of the castle of Banashala in Kashmir successfully used boulders against the troops of Jayasimha (*r.*1128–49):

> The royal troops were throwing stones from throwing machines, showers of arrows and various [other] missiles. And those in the castle defended themselves by rolling down stones. The royal army, though large, could not attack those in the castle, while stones were falling and arrows marked with Bhikshu's name … Notwithstanding their great number they were so repulsed by the hail of stones from those [in the castle] that they became convinced of this [undertaking] not being achievable by sheer prowess. The heads which the stones carried off from the bodies of brave soldiers, appeared, with their streams of blood, like beehives [thrown down by stone-hits], from the tops of trees with bees rising from them.[3]

Boulders could be round or a stretched oval shape. They were stored on the walls beforehand and shaped, time permitting, to a more or less rounded form so that they could be rolled from one place to another. At the peak of battle, however, any stone could be used, and sometimes buildings were purposely demolished for this purpose.

Before locking themselves inside a fortress, the defenders often engaged in battle outside the fortress walls. So the defenders of Brahamanabad went out of the gate to the drum-roll every day for six months and fought with the army of Muhammad Kasim from dawn till sunset. When the defenders found further resistance useless, they often tried to leave the fortress unseen, through a secret exit.

The siege of Chittorgarh in 1303 was the most famous, romantic and tragic siege of the period. Ala-ud-din Khalji, Sultan of Delhi, headed the siege himself. Not only did Ala-ud-din manage to successfully repulse the Mongol invasions, which reached their peak during his rule, but he also conquered new territory. Ala-ud-din was so proud of his conquests that he assumed the title of *Sikander Sani* ('Second Alexander', the first being Alexander the Great).

At the beginning of the 14th century Ala-ud-din sent out three armies of conquest: one to the Deccan, another to the Gujarat and the final one to Rajasthan (Rajputana). He commanded the Rajasthan army himself, and approached Chittorgarh, capital of the Mewar principality, in 1303. The ruler of Chittorgarh, Rana Rattan Singh, had a wife, Padmini, whose beauty made her

---

3 Kalhana's *Rajatarangini*, VIII, 1677–78, 1685–86

This palace in Chittorgarh was the home of Rani Padmini, the beautiful wife of Rana Rattan Singh, ruler of Mewar.

famous far beyond the boundaries of the principality. Legend has it that Ala-ud-din wished to seize Chittorgarh not only for the sake of expanding his borders, but also to take possession of the beautiful Padmini, and that was why he had placed himself at the head of the army. Whatever the reason, Ala-ud-din besieged the powerful hill castle. After a long, futile siege Ala-ud-din resorted to a ruse. He sent a letter to the rana promising to take his army back to Delhi if he was allowed to cast a glance at the rana's fair wife.

While this would not demean a European woman, it was unthinkable for a Rajput woman, especially a queen or princess, to reveal her face to a strange man. The Rajputs, however, were exhausted by the siege and wanted peace no less than Ala-ud-din did. After long negotiations it was agreed that Ala-ud-din should only be allowed to see Padmini's reflection in the mirror. He was let into the castle and brought to Padmini's palace. The palace, situated on the bank of a lake, can still be seen in Chittorgarh. Rani Padmini stood inside her palace with her back to the window and Ala-ud-din was able to have a look at the reflection of her beautiful face in a series of specially placed mirrors. His passion flared up. He ordered his soldiers to seize Rattan Singh while he was escorting him out of the gate, and demanded the beautiful queen in exchange for the ruler of Mewar.

The Rajputs devised a cunning plan to liberate their master. Padmini pretended to accept the offer of the Delhi sultan on condition that she should be accorded all the honours due to her high status. She demanded 700 covered palanquins for her court ladies and maidservants. Her demand fulfilled, she arrived at the enemy camp. However, instead of a lady, each palanquin concealed an armed Rajput soldier and weapons for the six men who carried the palanquin. Thus Padmini arrived at the enemy camp accompanied by 700 warriors and 4,200 warrior-porters and demanded to be allowed to say goodbye to her husband. As soon as she was brought to him, the Rajputs drew their arms, liberated their master and his wife, and fought their way back to the castle. The attack was so unexpected that Ala-ud-din's soldiers offered no resistance despite their considerable superiority in numbers. Soon, however, they rushed in pursuit, and nearly all the brave Rajputs died covering the retreat of their master.

Ala-ud-din was furious and besieged Chittorgarh again, intent on revenge. Having lost its best defenders in the liberation of Rattan Singh and Padmini, the castle could not withstand the attack. When this became obvious to the defenders, the Rajput women, led by Rani Padmini, performed the rite of self-immolation (*jauhar*) while the men came out of the castle to engage in their last fight to death (*shaka*). The 19th-century historian Colonel James Tod amassed a great deal of information about Rajasthan in the 19th century, and this is his account:

> Awful sacrifice was to precede this act of self devotion, in that horrible rite of 'jauhar' where the females are immolated to preserve them from pollution or captivity. The funeral pyre was lighted within the great subterranean retreat, in chambers impervious to the light of day and the defenders of Chittor beheld in procession the queens, their own wives and daughters to the number of several thousands. The fair Padmini closed the throng and they were conveyed to the cavern and the opening closed upon them, leaving them to find security from dishonour in the devouring fire.

The Rana then called his devoted clans, for whom life had no longer any charms. They threw open the portals and descended to the plains and with a reckless despair carried death or met it in the crowded ranks of Ala-ud-din. The Tatar conqueror took possession of an inanimate capital, strewed with brave defenders, the smoke yet issuing from the recesses where lay consumed the once fair object of his desire. And since this devoted day the cavern has been sacred: no eye has penetrated its gloom. Thus fell the celebrated capital in the round of conquest of Khalji, one of the most vigorous and warlike sovereigns who have occupied the throne of India.

It is thought that the *jauhar* was performed in the underground chambers of the palace; it was later rebuilt and is now called the Rana Kumbha's Palace. The entrance to the cavern is still closed. Indeed, Rajput women resorted to *jauhar* so often when a castle was doomed that the rite is almost a typical finale in the drama of a besieged Rajput castle. Twice again Chittorgarh saw *jauhar* performed inside its walls – when besieged by the sultan of Gujarat in 1535, and again by the Emperor Akbar in 1568.

While the women were committing *jauhar*, the Rajput men were engaged in their last fight, or *shaka*. They had no right to return, whether victorious or defeated – they were either to fall in battle or commit suicide. *Shaka* was not really fought in order to win, but to kill as many enemies as possible and then be killed. It was a form of self-sacrifice and, according to the canons of honour, the enemy could not appropriate what had been paid for so dearly. The land and castles for the sake of which *jauhar* and *shaka* were performed were to remain the property of the sacrificing clan and pass to the legal heirs. Therefore the clan took every possible measure to save the heir in a desperate situation. However sultans and later the Mughals and the British failed to appreciate the significance of these sacrifices and the traditional rules. Once he had captured Chittorgarh, Ala-ud-din handed it over to Khizer Khan to run and renamed it Khizerabad (about ten years later the castle was recaptured by Rajputs and regained its old name of Chittor).

Before engaging in a *shaka*, a Rajput performed his ablutions and drew the signs of *cakra* and *shankha* on his body in red paint. Then he put on saffron-coloured clothes (the colour saffron is sacred in Hinduism) and covered his head with a special crown called a *mor*, a kind of turban decorated with gems. A Rajput could only wear this turban twice in his life – at his wedding and going to *shaka*, and he could not put it on until all the women of the clan had died in the *jauhar*. The crown symbolized both a betrothal and the unity of the warriors going to death with the heavenly Apsara maidens. It is uncertain when the ritual acquired its final touch and Rajputs began to wear the saffron-coloured clothes generally associated with members of ascetic communities in the Hindu culture – probably in the 13th century. Before that time a warrior going to his death looked different – his tousled hair was sprinkled with ashes, he was armed with a trident and an axe as well as other weapons.

Rani Mahal (on the left) and Hammir Mahal (on the right) in Ranthambhor Castle. These two palaces adjoin each other and were dumb witnesses to the stormy events of the siege laid to the castle by the army of Ala-ud-din Khalji in 1300–01. When it became clear that the castle was doomed, the Rajput women performed the gruesome ceremony of self-immolation by fire (*jauhar*) in Rani Mahal. Hammir Mahal was the palace of Hammir Deo, ruler of Ranthambhor, who opened the gate and led the surviving Rajputs to their last battle with Ala-ud-din's army. Fronting the palaces is Padmala Pond, named after Hammir's daughter who, at the approach of the enemy, committed suicide by throwing herself into this pond.

The siege of Chittorgarh, 1303

Legend has it that Ala-ud-din Khalji, Sultan of Delhi, was so struck by the beauty of Rani Padmini, wife of Rana Rattan Singh, ruler of Chittorgarh, that he made up his mind to take possession of her at all costs and himself led an army to Rajasthan. His first attempt at besieging the castle failed. Then he managed to capture Rana Rattan Singh by guile, declaring that he would only set him free in exchange for Padmini. Disguised as ladies of Padmini's court and her housemaids, the Rajputs succeeded in infiltrating Ala-ud-din's camp and rescued their lord by force. The enraged sultan laid siege to Chittorgarh again. When it became clear that the castle had no chance of survival, all the women, led by Padmini, performed the rite of self-immolation by fire (*jauhar*). Their menfolk opened the castle gate and came out to die in their last fight, or *shaka*, from which they had no right to come back alive.

The fate of the castles

There is nothing a historian would like better than an opportunity to explore a deserted city, ideally one that perished dramatically and suddenly like Pompeii after the eruption of Mount Vesuvius. The same is true of scholars studying fortifications. What they dream of are the fortifications of a site that was suddenly abandoned and left untouched, unaltered by subsequent generations. Although no Indian cities were suddenly destroyed by a sudden disaster like Pompeii, there are several which were abandoned due to the ambitions of their rulers. Unfortunately for a modern researcher, they are not numerous and are mainly represented by the old cities of Delhi: Qila Rai Pithora, Siri, Tughluqabad, Jahanpanah and Firuzabad. Although the precise date when each of these cities was abandoned is uncertain, it presumably coincided with the appearance of the new city when most of the population moved and left the old one to decay. There are exceptions, however. The walls of Jahanpanah, for example, were erected to protect the suburbs of the cities of Qila Rai Pithora and Siri, which must have been populated at that time. Nevertheless, the fortifications of old cities were never rebuilt and that is of paramount importance to us.

Very few castles have survived unchanged since the early Middle Ages or even since the 14th–15th centuries: most of those built in the 10th–15th centuries were later rebuilt and altered. Castles were still used as living quarters until the 19th–20th centuries, and so were continually modified. Even now, some of them are private property.

When studying fortifications it is useful to be able to identify the features characteristic of earlier defences as distinct from those added later. With the growing popularity of firearms, the parapets of many castles were modified or even entirely rebuilt in order to accommodate handguns and cannon. Small square openings, seen for example in the walls of Ranthambhor Castle, were designed for handguns. Large square embrasures were made in nearly every castle for light cannon. In some cases, which are mainly typical of the 18th century, the parapet and walls were completely rebuilt on the pattern of European gun emplacement. However, the Indians rarely resorted to such a radical method. They were generally content with cutting square embrasures for light cannon and erecting solid pedestals for heavy cannon beyond a wall. These wide, low platforms were circular or square in shape and all had a slope along which cannon could be easily pulled up.

Medieval walls of Indian castles were not designed for mounting heavy large-calibre cannon. With the spread of gunpowder artillery, square or round gun pedestals began to be built near the walls. The pedestals had an upward incline to make it easier to mount a cannon. The upper town of Bidar has three round tower-like pedestals named Black, Red and Long.

The castles today

Visiting India, except for the foothills of the Himalayas, is best in winter and spring, or, to be exact, from January to May when the temperature is not too high and rains are rare. Summer is very hot in many regions: in the desert of Rajasthan the temperature may rise to 48 degrees centigrade in the shade. Rain is widespread during monsoons in summer and autumn.

It is worth renting a car with a driver, which allows a traveller sufficient freedom of movement. A car with a driver can be hired from almost every tourist agency for a cost of £10–15 (about $20) a day for trips within the city bounds and £35–40 ($60–70) for a long journey (petrol and bed and board for the driver included). Renting a car without a driver can be troublesome due to the busy nature of the roads in India and the peculiarities of the traffic regulations.

When asking the way, remember that all the ancient and medieval fortifications, whether well preserved or lying in ruins, are commonly known as forts in India. A local guide will offer his services at the entrance of practically every castle. Most of them are authorized guides though one can occasionally come across a pure enthusiast.

Listed below are the major medieval Indian castles whose fortifications mostly date from that time. Castles founded during that period but considerably rebuilt later will be covered in a later book.

Each description begins with the common name of the place where the castle is situated; the castle usually has the same name, but if it is different, it is mentioned in the text. Other names that may be encountered in guides or other books are given in brackets. The name of the modern Indian state where the castle is situated is added to make it easier to find the castle on the map.

Bidar, Karnataka
Bidar lies about 130km north-west of Hyderabad. Apart from interesting fortifications, Bidar houses several palaces, a mosque built in 1327, a 15th-century *madrasa* and the residence of the commandant of the fortress. The circular tower Chaubara, a former watchtower, survives and can be seen at a crossroads in the lower town.

Chittorgarh (Chitorgarh, Chittaurgarh, Chittoregarh, Chittor Castle), Rajasthan
About 115km north-east of Udaipur, Chittorgarh's fortifications and three palaces are well worth visiting. The 22.8m Tower of Fame, built supposedly in the 12th century, and the 37.2m Tower of Victory built in 1458–68 to commemorate the victory over Mahmud Khalji of Malwa in 1440, are noteworthy, too. The castle also houses several Jain temples and a small museum with a collection of sculptures, bas-reliefs and medieval weapons.

The Tower of Victory built in Chittorgarh in 1458–68 in memory of the victory over Mahmud Khalji of Malwa in 1440. The tower has nine storeys and is 37.2m high. A visitor can climb the staircase made inside the tower up to the top and view the surroundings from the height of a bird's flight.

Ruins of the walls of Lal Kot (Red Fortress). The fortress was built c.1060 by King Anangapal of the Rajput Tomar clan. In 1180 Lal Kot became part of the defences of the first city of Delhi, Qila Rai Pithora, and its fortifications were rebuilt.

Cuttak, Orissa
Situated about 35km north of Bhubaneshwar, Cuttak is noted for the ruins of the 13th- or 14th-century Barabati Castle. The large round tower was built in 1750.

Dabhoi, Gujarat
Dabhoi lies 25km south-east of Vadodara. Only the western and part of the northern wall and four gates of this 13th-century castle, once a fine example of Hindu architecture, survive.

Daulatabad, Maharashtra
Daulatabad ('City of Fortune'), originally known as Deogiri or Devagiri ('Hill of Gods'), is situated 13km east of Aurangabad. It is one of the most powerful and best-preserved castles in India. Little remains of the outer fortifications that once surrounded the city, but as if to make up for it, the three lines of defence that protected the citadel are almost intact. The outer line, consisting of a double wall with moats in front and between the walls, is especially impressive. The gate in this wall is also marked by a complex structure, with a barbican and two successive courts. However, it is at the entrance to the citadel that one is hit by the most interesting structural decision. The first obstacle here is a moat with a permanent bridge, flooded in case of emergency. Further, the road passes past a tower, through a cavern, across an open court and finally through a tunnel that could be filled with a suffocating gas.

Delhi
Delhi is traditionally believed to occupy the site of the legendary town of *The Mahabharata*, Indraprastha, and excavations on the territory of Purana Qila confirm the existence of a settlement here about 3,000 years ago. The seven medieval cities of Delhi are well known, but there were really several more. An ambitious ruler seeking to immortalize his name would abandon an old city and found a new one nearby, named after himself.

Qila Rai Pithora (Fortress of Rai Pithora), or the first city of Delhi, was built c.1180 by Rai Pithora Prithviraja. A fortress known as Lal Kot (Red Fortress), which had existed here since c.1060, was included in the defences of the new city, forming a citadel on its south-west side. The Lal Kot fortifications were then substantially rebuilt. The rubble-built walls of both Lal Kot and Qila Rai Pithora are strengthened at short intervals with semicircular towers. There was a ditch in front of the walls of both fortresses, but it only partially survives. Lal Kot had seven gates, of which the Ghazni, Sohan and Ranjit Gates are known.

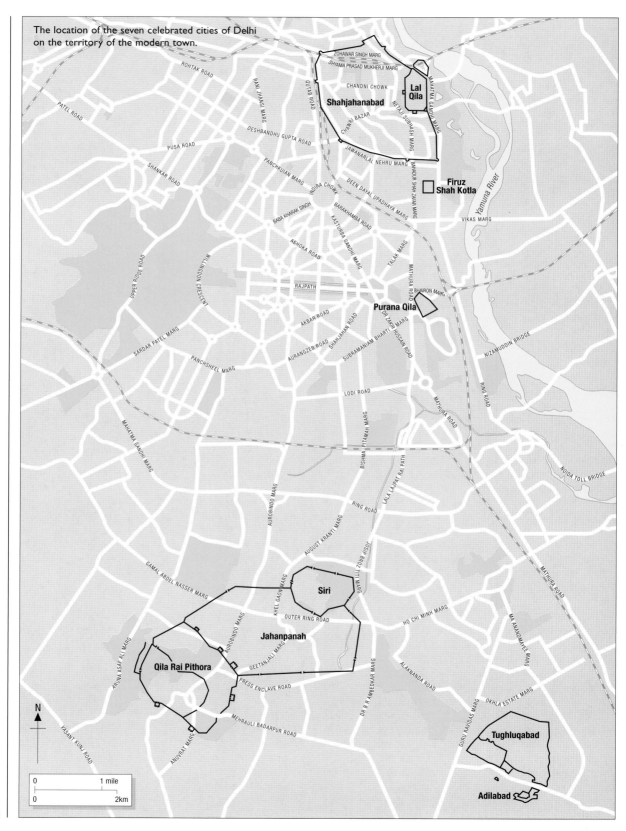

The location of the seven celebrated cities of Delhi on the territory of the modern town.

Shahjahanabad

Lal Qila

Firuz Shah Kotla

Purana Qila

Siri

Jahanpanah

Qila Rai Pithora

Tughluqabad

Adilabad

ZOHAWAR SINGH MARG
SHYAMA PRASAD MUKHERJI MARG
CHANDNI CHOWK
CHANRI BAZAR
JAWANARLAL NEHRU MARG
ROHTAK ROAD
QUTAB ROAD
RANI JHANSI MARG
PATEL ROAD
DESHBANDHU GUPTA ROAD
PUSA ROAD
SHANKAR ROAD
PANCHKUIAN MARG
INDIRA CHOWK
DEEN DAYAL UPADHAYA MARG
MAHATMA GANDHI MARG
NETAJI SUBHASH MARG
BAHADUR SHAH ZAFAR MARG
VIKAS MARG
Yamuna River
BABA KHARAK SINGH
BARAKHAMBA ROAD
KASTURBA GANDHI MARG
ASHOKA ROAD
TALAK MARG
MATHURA ROAD
BHAIRON MARG
UPPER RIDGE ROAD
WILLINGDON CRESCENT
RAJPATH
AKBAR ROAD
SHINJHAN ROAD
DR ZAKIR HUSSAIN ROAD
NIZAMUDDIN BRIDGE
SARDAR PATEL MARG
PANCHSHEEL MARG
AURANGZEB ROAD
SUBRAMANIAM BHARTI ROAD
MATHURA ROAD
RING ROAD
LODI ROAD
NOIDA TOLL BRIDGE
MAHATMA GANDHI MARG
BISHMA PITAMAH MARG
LALA LAJPAT RAI PATH
AUROBINDO MARG
AUGUST KRANTI MARG
RING ROAD
JOSIP BROZ TITO MARG
GAMAL ABDEL NASSER MARG
KHEL GAON MARG
OUTER RING ROAD
HO CHI MINH MARG
AUROBINDO MARG
GEETANJALI MARG
DR B R AMBEDKAR MARG
ALAKNANDA ROAD
ARUNA ASAF ALI MARG
PRESS ENCLAVE ROAD
MA ANANDMAYEE MARG
MATHURA ROAD
VASANT KUNJ ROAD
MEHRAULI BADARPUR ROAD
GURU RAVIDAS MARG
OKHLA ESTATE MARG
ANUVRAT MARG

N

0   1 mile
0   2km

54

Barbicans defended a number of the gates. Out of 13 gates at Qila Rai Pithora, only the remains of the Hauz-Rani, Barka and Budaun Gates survive.

The fortifications of Qila Rai Pithora and Lal Kot can be seen along the sides of Delhi road (near the tenth milestone), Gurgaon road (close to Adham Khan's tomb) and Badarpur or Tughluqabad road (about one mile from Qutb Minar). There are also some remains of the walls on either side of the road right after it passes Adhchini village. However, vast sections of the walls are hidden in the thickets and it is difficult to find them without a guide. The rings of the walls are clearly visible from the famous Qutb Minar, the five-storeyed Victory Tower and minaret 72.3m high.

Siri, or the second city of Delhi, was built in 1303 by Ala-ud-din Khalji. A once-flourishing town, it was ravaged by Timur and shortly after that fell into decay. In the 16th century, under Sher Shah Sur, stones from the fortress walls were widely used as building material, so only the basements of the towers and small sections of the walls survive. These can be seen near the Siri Fort Auditorium and the adjacent village of Shahpur Jat. Judging by the preserved sections, the walls had three or four tiers of fire: probably two rows of loopholes from the mural galleries and two from parapet level (downwards through loopholes under the parapet and right ahead through crenels or loopholes in merlons). Flame-shaped merlons probably made their earliest appearance here.

Tughluqabad, or the third city of Delhi, is situated in the south-east part of Delhi, about 8km from Qutb Minar on the Mehrauli–Badarpur road. In 1325 the small fortress of Adilabad was added to Tughluqabad. To the east of Adilabad, ruins of the small fortress Nai-ka-Kot ('Barber Fortress') can be seen on a hillock, which was apparently Muhammad bin Tughluq's private residence before Adilabad was built. Tughluqabad was inhabited for only a few years before being abandoned when Muhammad bin Tughluq built Jahanpanah.

Jahanpanah, or the fourth city of Delhi, is situated between Qila Rai Pithora and Siri, which were connected by defensive walls. The city was abandoned shortly after its construction when the capital was transferred to Daulatabad in 1328. Very little of the walls survives, but scarce ruins can be seen to the north of Chiragh-Delhi and Begampur villages and the Indian Institute of Technology, to the south of Khirki Mosque and 800m to the east of it, at the Satpula weir.

Firuz Shah Tughluq built Firuzabad, or the fifth city of Delhi, in 1354. Urban fortifications do not survive, but the ruins of the citadel called Firuz Shah Kotla are impressive indeed. The citadel comprised three walled enclosures connected by a common eastern wall that used to reach the river. The central enclosure is larger than the other two and includes the palace complex, together with the Ashokan pillar. The northern enclosure can only be traced in part, having been absorbed by modern buildings. The southern enclosure now encompasses the

Adilabad. This fortress, small as compared with Tughluqabad, adjoins the latter on its southern side. It was constructed by Ghiyath-ud-din Tughluq's son, Muhammad bin Tughluq, in c.1325.

55

A wall of Firuz Shah Kotla, the citadel of Firuzabad, the so-called fifth city of Delhi. The lower row of loopholes is on a level with a mural gallery, while the upper row was under the parapet that does not survive.

Vikramnagar colony. Two round towers flank the main entrance, situated on the western side of the central enclosure, but the barbican commanding the approaches to the gate does not survive. The walls of Firuz Shah Kotla are fairly well preserved apart from the battlemented parapet. The walls now have two rows of loopholes: halfway up the wall on a level with the mural gallery, and under the parapet.

The sixth city, Dinpanah, with its citadel Purana Qila, and the seventh city, Shahjahanabad, with its citadel Lal Qila, both dating from a later period, are not considered in this book.

Firuzabad, Karnataka
The impressive ruins of the city supposedly founded by Firuz Shah Bahmani in about 1400 and abandoned in the mid-15th century, lie 28km south of Gulbarga on the east bank of the Bhima River. Formidable stone walls reinforced by towers and four gates encompass a vast area built over with palaces, mosques, houses and the oldest baths in the Deccan.

Gaur, West Bengal
The fortifications of this city, which prospered in the 15th century lie 8km south-west of English Bazaar (*Ingraj Bazar*). Nothing but strong earth ramparts and two gates survive. Dakhil Darwaza, built of small red brick and highly decorated, is most attractive. Within the enclosure is a palace fenced by a brick wall.

Gingee (Jinjee, locally called Senji), Tamil Nadu
Situated 132km south-west of Chennai (formerly Madras) and about 60km north-west of Pondicherry (Puduchcheri), this castle is one of the most impressive in India. Its fortifications occupy three hills – Krishnagiri, Rajagiri and Chandragiri (or Chandradurg). Defensive walls connect these hills and the fortifications form a triangle. The highest hill, Rajagiri, houses the citadel enclosed in three additional defensive lines. Seven gates defend the route to the citadel. The construction of the fortifications began in 1442 and finished in the next century.

Golconda, Andhra Pradesh
Golconda ('Shepherd's Hill') lies about 9km west of Hyderabad and has three lines of defence: the outer, urban fortification; the middle wall surrounding the base of the hill on which the citadel sits; and the innermost wall following the contours of the highest ridge. The rulers of the Qutb Shahi dynasty built most of the fortifications between 1518 and 1580. However, the innermost wall of the citadel,

Citadel walls in Golconda. Faced with solid stone blocks free of mortar, these walls are skilfully attached to the huge stone clods of the rock. Two box machicolations, each lying on three corbels, can be seen near the gate.

laid of massive stone blocks without mortar, was undoubtedly built prior to that period, probably in the 12th–14th centuries. In 1724 an extension (Naya Qila or New Fortress) was built to the north-east of the city; the most curious object of its walls is the Nine-Lobed Tower. Among other interesting features are embrasures between merlons, covered with horizontal and vertical stone partitions so that only small holes for handguns are left; semicircular mantlets fronting the Bala Hisar and Banjara gates; and also a great many box machicolations characteristic of the Deccan on the walls and towers. The total extent of the Golconda walls, including nine gates and 87 towers, is about 9km.

Gulbarga, Karnataka
Founded in the 14th century, the castle is encircled by a strong double wall and a wide ditch. There were two gates: the western gate fronted by a ruined barbican and four consecutive courts is best preserved. The outer gate is strengthened with anti-elephant spikes of an unusual design: each round hub is crowned with four spirally twisted spikes. A six-tower rectangular donjon is a unique feature of the castle.

Gwalior, Madhya Pradesh
The castle stands on a rocky hill, towering 91m above the surrounding countryside. The fortifications date back to the 10th–17th centuries and the eastern gate complex is the most interesting of them. Out of the six palaces, the splendid Man Mandir, built between 1486 and 1516 by Raja Man Singh of the Tomar dynasty, deserves special attention as a most remarkable and interesting example of an early Hindu palace.

Kumbhalgarh, Rajasthan
About 70km north of Udaipur, this castle was built by Rana Kumbha in 1443–58 and is one of the most impressive in Rajasthan. The walls, strengthened by formidable towers at regular intervals, stretch over many kilometres. The wall-walk is so wide that six horsemen are said to have been able to ride abreast along it. The citadel sits on the summit of the hill, which is belted with walls, and the fortifications have many peculiar features: a solid talus of the walls and particularly towers; hooked spikes on some of the gates; and a variety of unusually shaped loopholes (there are crosslet slit loopholes and some in which three or four outside openings correspond to one opening on the inside).

Hathi Gate and Man Mandir Palace in Gwalior Castle. Hathi means 'elephant' and the gate received its name (Elephant Gate) from the statue of an elephant with a drover that used to stand in front of the gate. King Man Singh, the builder of Man Mandir Palace, is supposed to have sat on that elephant himself.

Madurai, Tamil Nadu
The city's fortifications once consisted of a double wall and a moat, supposedly dating from the 14th century, but only fragments of the walls survive today.

Mandu, Madhya Pradesh
Mandu is 40km south-east of Dhar and the immensely long outer walls follow the contours of the plateau. Inside, there are two fortified enclosures where the royal palaces are located. The fortifications were mainly built in the first half of the 15th century by the Sultan of Malwa, although the crown of the hill was fortified much earlier.

Panhala (Panhalgarh), Maharashtra
Lying 19km north-west of Kolhapur, Panhala was one of the most important castles in the Deccan. The defensive wall, built mainly in the 15th century, reflects the contours of the hill and extends about 7km. Two of the three gates survive, and the castle houses a 12th-century citadel.

Parenda, Maharashtra
This strong, but relatively small castle, built in about the mid-15th century, lies 29km west of Barsi. A rectangular site is enclosed within a powerful double wall with towers and box machicolations.

Purandhar, Maharashtra
Lying 32km south-east of Pune, this hill castle once was among the strongest castles in the Deccan. Its fortifications mainly date from the 15th century.

Raichur, Karnataka
The fortifications of Raichur comprise a citadel and urban defences. The citadel sits on a hill, in a limited, almost square, enclosed site. The most interesting structure

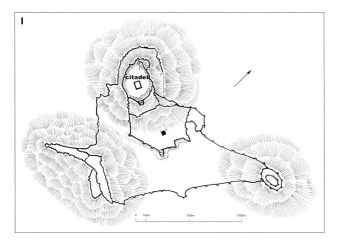

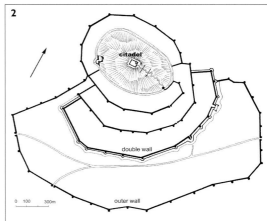

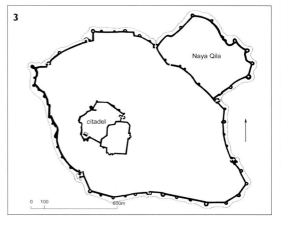

Layout of fortifications
(after S. Toy):
(1) Gingee, 15th–16th centuries;
(2) Daulatabad, 11th–17th centuries;
(3) Golconda, 12th–18th centuries.

here is a pavilion, which is crowned with rectangular merlons uncharacteristic of Indian fortification. A single winding road, consisting of a series of steps, reaches the citadel. About halfway up, the road is barred with a wall and a gate. The base of the hill is surrounded by a wall built of huge stone blocks without mortar and apparently dating back to the 13th century. The urban defences were built in the 16th century and consist of a moat and a wall with towers of several different shapes (round, square and twin-lobed).

Ranthambhor (Ranthambhore), Rajasthan

Some 19km north-east of Sawai Madhopur, in Ranthambhor National Park, the imposing ruins of the castle crown an isolated rock 213m high. The fortifications mainly date from the 13th century, but were rebuilt in the 15th century and later. Square loopholes were designed for firearms and are a revealing example of later rebuilds. The fortifications are fairly well preserved. Whole families of monkeys meet a visitor at the gate eager to become your guides about the castle precincts, posing at, by and on the sights. About 40km east of Sawai Madhopur, also within Ranthambhor National Park, are the ruins of Khandar Castle, which was built prior to the 12th century. The main entrance to the castle is through three gates. On the way one can admire Jain idols. A red stone sculpture of an elephant welcomes you at the main gate.

Shivner, Maharashtra

Situated 80km north of Puna, near Junnar, this 14th-century castle sits on the summit of a hill surrounded by walls. Seven gates bar a long, steep and winding route from the foot of the hill to the summit. The walls and gates are fairly well preserved. Inside, there is a restored house, the birthplace of the Maratha leader Shivaji.

Thanjavur (Tanjore), Tamil Nadu

The fortifications that once encircled the city and temple area only survive in a few places. They stand to their full height on the western and southern extremities of the city, while in other parts there are no more than earthen ramparts, once the core of the walls. The townsfolk later pilfered many of the original stones. The fortifications consisted of a double wall strengthened with towers and a moat. Only one of the six gates has been preserved. The fortifications were presumably built in the 14th century, but were also repaired later.

Bala Hisar Gate in Golconda. The gate itself is screened by a semicircular barbican, which is not actually connected to the citadel walls and was designed to protect the gate against an attack with elephants or siege engines. The barbican, like the gate itself, has plenty of the box machicolations so characteristic of military architecture of the Deccan.

Vijayanagar (Vijayanagara), Karnataka

The impressive ruins of the central part of the city that was the capital of the Vijayanagar Empire from 1336 to 1565 lie between the villages of Hampi in the north and Kamalapuram in the south. Hampi is about 13km north-east of Hospet, which is about 60km west of the city of Bellary. The city was enclosed with seven defensive rings. The outer ring ran about 3km south of Hospet, the second just to the south of Hospet, and the third through the town itself. The fourth and fifth lines were to the south and north of the present village Malpannagudi. The sixth line skirted the northern bund of the Kamalapuram tank, ran through the village of Kadiramapuram in the north-western direction and then turned almost straight to the north. The seventh, innermost and best-preserved line edges the central part of the town with its temples and the ruins of the citadel.

Warangal, Andhra Pradesh

The citadel, built in the mid-13th century, is fairly well preserved and an excellent example of Hindu architecture. Square in plan, it is provided with a gate in the middle of each side. The gates all have the same structure, consisting of a barbican and two successive courts. There are two sculptures of lions fronting the outer gateway of the western gate. An earthen rampart, apparently built in the 8th century AD, encloses the citadel and the city and has a powerful stone gate and a barbican. Built by Muslim rulers, the gate dates from a later period than the citadel.

Bibliography and further reading

Archaeological Remains, Monuments & Museums, 2 vols (New Delhi, 1996, first published 1964)

Bhakari, S.K., *Indian Warfare: An Appraisal and Tactics of War in Early Medieval Period* (New Delhi, 1981)

Davies P., *The Penguin Guide to the Monuments of India. Volume II: Islamic, Rajput, European* (London, 1989)

Devakunjari, D., *Hampi* (New Delhi, 1998)

Fass, Virginia, *The Forts of India* (London, 1986)

Kalhana, *Rajatarangini. A Chronicle of the Kings of Kashmir* (transl. M.A. Stein), 2 vols. (Delhi, 1961)

Kamalapur, J.N., *The Deccan Forts. A study in the Art of Fortification in Medieval India* (Bombay, 1961)

Kautilya , *The Arthashastra* (transl. L.N. Rangarajan) (New Delhi, 1992)

Khan, I.A., *Gunpowder and Firearms. Warfare in Medieval India* (New Delhi & Oxford, 2004)

The Mahabharata: An English Version Based on Selected Verses (transl. Chakravarthi V. Narasimhan) (New York, 1965)

Nicolle, D., *New Vanguard 69: Medieval Siege Weapons (2), Byzantium, the Islamic World & India AD 476–1526* (Oxford, 2003)

Partington, J.R., *A History of Greek Fire and Gunpowder* (Baltimore & London, 1999)

Paul, E.J., *'By My Sword and Shield'. Traditional Weapons of the Indian Warrior* (New Delhi, 1995)

Ramayana (transl. W. Buck) (Berkeley, 1981)

Rigveda (transl. R.T.H. Griffith) (Livingston, 1986)

Sarkar, J.N., *The Art of War in Medieval India* (New Delhi, 1984)

Sharma, Y.D., *Delhi and Its Neighbourhood* (New Delhi, 2001)

Singh, A.P., *Forts and Fortifications in India, with Special Reference to Central India* (Delhi, 1993)

Singh, S.D., *Ancient Indian Warfare* (Delhi, 1997)

Tadgell, C., *The History of Architecture in India* (London, 1998)

Tod, James, *Annals and Antiquities of Rajasthan* (London, 1950)

Toy, S., *The Fortified Cities of India* (London, 1965)

Toy, S., *The Strongholds of India* (London, 1957)

Uspenskaya, E.N., *Rajputy. Rytsari srednevekovoi Indii* (Rajputs. Knights of Medieval India) (St Petersburg, 2000)

Verma, Amrit, *Forts of India* (New Delhi, 2003)

Further reading

Until now, Sidney Toy's *The Strongholds of India* and *The Fortified Cities of India* remain the best guidebooks for anyone who wants to visit Indian castles. The second title is a sequel to and elaboration of the first, and both contain general plans of the fortresses, as well as detailed diagrams of particular parts of them (gates, parapets, and so on).

A good historical background for many castles is offered in Amrit Verma's *Forts of India*, although there are relatively few descriptions of fortifications in this book. Virginia Fass's book, *The Forts of India*, is an excellently illustrated guide.

The history and fortifications of individual castles are well described in the following books: J.N. Kamalapur, *The Deccan Forts. A Study in the Art of Fortification in Mediaeval India* and A.P. Singh, *Forts and Fortifications in India, with Special Reference to Central India (Madhya Pradesh)*. As their titles show, each book deals with castles of a particular district, although the last of them offers a general review of fortifications as well.

Chapters on fortifications and siege warfare of the period in question are to be found in S.K. Bhakari, *Indian Warfare. An Appraisal and Tactics of War in Early Medieval Period*, and J.N. Sarkar, *The Art of War in Medieval India*.

Those reading in Russian are welcome to read my book: K.S. Nossov, *Zamki i kreposti Indii* (Castles and Fortresses of India) (St Petersburg, 2006).

Glossary

List of abbreviations:
[Eur] – term of European fortification
[Hin] – Hindi
[Raj] – Rajasthani
[San] – Sanskrit
Where the source is not indicated, the term is a borrowing from or derivative of an Arabic, Farsi, Urdu, Turkish or one of many local languages and dialects; the latter numbered about 225 in India in 1901.

ab-durga (āb-durga) [San] see *jala-durga*

airina-durga [San] a fortress built on barren saline soil or fens saturated with saline water and strewn with thorny bushes

antapala-durga (antapāla-durga) [San] lit. 'fortress for border guarding'; a frontier fortress

antardvipa-durga (antardvīpa-durga) [San] lit. 'island fortress'; a fortress surrounded on all sides with the waters of a sea or river

attalaka (aṭṭālaka) [San] tower

audaka-durga [San] lit. 'water fortress' (see *jala-durga*)

ayudha-durga (āyudha-durga) [San] lit. 'fortress with weapons'; a fortress well fortified, armed and equipped for defensive and offensive operations

bala-durga [San] lit. 'strong fortress' or 'fortress with men' (see *nri-durga*)

barbican [Eur] a fortification designed for the defence of a gate or bridge leading to a gate

berm [Eur] a horizontal strip of land between the ditch and wall preventing earth crumbling into the ditch and wall collapsing

bhavana [San] a house, a palace

box machicolation [Eur] several openings – machicolations – placed in a small cabin projecting beyond the wall. A box machicolation may sit halfway up a wall, or at the summit, on parapet level; it may be uncovered or covered on the top. Extra loopholes were sometimes made in the front and side walls of the cabin

darvaza [Hin] a gate

darwar [Hin] a palace

deva-bhavana [San] lit. 'home of god', a temple

deva-durga [San] lit. 'gods' fortress'

dhanu-durga (dhanū-durga) [San] see dhanvana-durga

dhanvana-durga, dhanva-durga [San] lit. 'desert fortress'; a fortress in a desert

dhavalgriha (dhavalgṛha) [San] a complex of living quarters of a ruler in the palace

diwar [Hin] fortress wall

durga, durg [San] a fortress or castle

durga-pati [San] commandant of a fortress

dwimukha-durga [San] lit. 'double-gate fortress'

ekamukha-durga [San] lit. 'one-gate fortress'

garh [Raj] castle or fortress

giri-durga [San] lit. 'hill or mountain fortress'

giri-parshva-durga (giri-pārśva-durga) [San] lit. 'fortress at the side of a hill or mountain'; a fortress whose major structures and buildings stand on the sloping side of a hill (the summit of the hill is also defended by fortifications)

gopura [San] gate

guha-durga (guhā-durga) [San] lit. 'secluded, concealed fortress'; a plain fortress surrounded and protected by high, difficult mountains

gumma [Hin] a tower

howdah the seat on an elephant's back, sometimes canopied

jala-durga [San] lit. 'water fortress'; a fortress surrounded with water

jana-bhavana [San] lit. 'home of man'; the dwelling of a common man (as distinct from raja-bhavana and deva-bhavana)

jauhar, johar mass suicide by fire practised by Rajput women to escape dishonour at the hands of their captors

khanjana-durga (khañjana-durga) [San] a fortress standing on fens, surrounded with thorny bushes

kurma-durga (kūrma-durga) [San] lit. 'tortoise fortress'; a fortress built in a forest or at the foot of a hill and probably designed for effecting an ambush

machicolation [Eur] a loophole, made at the top of a wall or tower, commanding the foot of a wall. Such loopholes can be isolated (slot machicolation) or may be arranged along the entire top of the wall, put on corbels

mahi-durga (mahī-durga) [San] lit. 'earth fortress'

maidan vacant space or square at the front of fortifications

mandir, mandira [San] a house, palace, temple or hall

mardana men's apartments in a palace

maru-durga [San] lit. 'desert fortress'; see *dhanvana-durga*

masjid a mosque

mishra-durga (miśra-durga) [San] lit. 'mixed fortress'

mrid-durga (mṛd-durga) [San] a fortress surrounded by earthen walls

nadi-durga (nadī-durga) [San] lit. 'river fortress'

nara-durga [San] see *nri-durga*

nirudaka-durga [San] lit. 'waterless fortress'; see *dhanvana-durga*

nri-durga (nṛ-durga) [San] lit. 'fortress with men'; a fortress defended by a large and loyal army boasting celebrated warriors

panka-durga (paṅka-durga) [San] lit. 'marsh fortress'; a fortress approaches to which are protected by fens or quicksands.

parigha-durga (parighā-durga) [San] a fortress surrounded with earth-and-stone or earth-and-brick walls over 12 cubits high

parikha (parikhā) [San] ditch

parna (parṇa) [San] merlon

parvata-durga (pārvata-durga) [San] lit. 'hill or mountain fortress'; see *giri-durga*

pol, pole [Hin] gate

prabha-durga (prabhā-durga) [San] lit. 'magnificent (powerful) fortress'; a fortress having several rings of solid walls, watch towers and so on

prakara (prākāra) [San] a fortress wall

prantara-durga (prāntara-durga) [San] a fortress on top of a mountain

pratoli (pratolī) [San] lit. 'wide road', 'main street'; a gate (see *gopura*)

pura, pur [San] a fortress or fortified city

pura-bhettarah (pura-bhettārah) [San] lit. 'destroyer of fortresses'; the phrase was frequently referred to elephants which were used as battering-rams for breaching gates and walls

qila [Hin] a castle or fortress

raja-bhavana [San] lit. 'king's home', a palace

ratha-durga [San] lit. 'chariot fortress'

shaka the Rajputs' last deadly fight

shala (śālā) [San] a fortress wall; also means 'home'

sthala-durga [San] lit. 'plain fortress'; a fortress encircled by artificial moats filled with water or river waters

sthambha-durga [San] a fortress in a jungle surrounded by tall trees with insufficient source of water

surunga (suruṅgā) [San] an underground passage, undermining.

talus [Eur] a sloped widening along the lower part of a wall or tower

tuk fortified complex of Jain temples

vana-durga [San] lit. 'arboreal fortress'

varksha-durga (vārksha-durga) [San] see *vrikshya-durga*

vrikshya-durga (vṛkshya-durga) [San] lit. 'wood castle'; see *vana-durga*

zenana women's apartments in a palace

Index

Figures in **bold** refer to illustrations.